LIVING
AWARE
&
INSPIRED

INTUITION, THE BIOENERGY FIELD,
MIND, AND EMOTIONS

HELEN PANKOWSKY, MD

Virginia

Published in the United States by WriteLife Publishing
(an imprint of Boutique of Quality Books Publishing Company, Inc.)
www.writelife.com

Printed in the United States of America
978-1-60808-207-0 (p)
978-1-60808-208-7 (e)
Library of Congress Control Number: 2018961942

Book design by Robin Krauss, www.bookformatters.com
Cover design by Marla Thompson, www.edgeofwater.com
Illustrations © 2017 Helen Pankowsky, MD All rights reserved
Image of Jimmy Durante from Wikicommons in the Public Domain.
Image of lobes of the brain— original: Henry Gray (1918) *Anatomy of the Human Body* from Wikicommons in the Public Domain.
Line art separators by Vecteezy, www.vecteezy.com

First editor: Olivia Swenson
Second editor: Caleb Guard

CONTENTS

PART I

INTUITION

PART II

THE HUMAN BIOENERGY FIELD

PART III

THE MIND-FIELD, EMOTIONS, BODY, AND SOUL

ACKNOWLEDGMENTS

There are no coincidences related to who comes into my life. Many people have helped and supported me in the process of writing this book, whether subtly or overtly. To thank everyone who has supported me would be a tome in itself, but I am compelled to acknowledge certain people. Many started as wonderful teachers—some without such intent—and ended as friends, mentors, or role models. The ones I have to thank for fulfilling this role are my patients, students, and all the skilled people who have enriched me. I am especially indebted to Valerie Hunt and Suzanne Lahl, my first guides to the relationship of the human bioenergy field, emotions, and the soul; to Harry Wilmer, MD, who showed me how to read the symbols, metaphors, and imagery within and outside; to Ming Xie and Weixsu Su, my extraordinary qigong and tai chi teachers, who have shown me the way of the Eastern mind, allowing me to integrate it with the Western; and to Brian Dailey, MD, my gentle, powerful, and compassionate Reiki teacher.

I am thankful for my friends and all the others who entered my life whether long-term or short, including my tai chi family, my colleagues, fellow healers and seekers. I am grateful for June Robinson, the most gifted healer I know and who believed in my capacity as an energy healer long before I did; Marjorie Brody for her friendship and advice on writing books and getting them out into the world; and for my friend-for-life Joan Zurakov, the only person in the world who can make me curse like a sailor and laugh uncontrollably as we unabashedly discuss our human foibles.

Many thanks to Terri Leidich, my publisher who gave the book a new life, Olivia Swenson, editor extraordinaire, and the behind-the-scenes staff of WriteLife Publishing.

I am immensely grateful to my family: my parents, Hanna and Jaime Pankowsky, for being my first teachers and for always supporting my endeavors; my son, Jacob Alonso, for his intelligence, technical expertise, his generous and compassionate heart, and for his incomparable humor; Liddy Morris, my lovely and brilliant daughter-in-law; and my husband, Dan Alonso, for being my rock, challenging me by playing devil's advocate, often to the point of infuriation (although sometimes forcing me to see a different perspective in order to make a change), never questioning my need to explore, cheering me up and cheering me on, and lovingly supporting me through the entire journey. I am grateful to all of you who have stood by me and supported me with your generosity and love.

PREFACE

At the age when we tend to ask questions, I thought how much easier my life would be if I simply lived an orthodox life, unquestioningly believing what I was taught and allowing my life to be structured by precepts determined by my family, culture, society, and religion. But I am not made of such stuff. I decided, as difficult as it was and continues to be, that I would rather make my way questioning beliefs than blindly going along with them.

Somewhere around my eighth year, I had my first glimpse of what it meant to be human within the greatness of the universe. I was in bed when I saw myself lying in my bed, in my room, in our house, on our street, in the neighborhood, in the town, in the state, in the country, in the world, in the solar system, in the universe among the stars—and all this with a sense that there was a beyond I couldn't see. It felt as if I had been rising, ascending, soaring into something awesome, amazing, mysterious. Startled by the immensity of the experience, I was jolted back into my bed.

In my home, science, history, and intellect were valued more than mysticism, so I kept the experience to myself. The only way I could make sense of it then was to see it as a reflection of my smallness in the vastness of the universe. Yet there was something profound in the idea that even if I was small, I could still see and feel an unknown so large.

In addition, the experience was something I was not ready to comprehend; it has taken me years to do so. What I experienced that night was an insight into what I have come to believe is our truth. It was a manifestation of what we are—divine humans. We have the vulnerability of a physical body *and* the capacity and power of the soul and the divine. When we embrace both our human vulnerability and our divine power, we are best able to live with expanded consciousness and to live an inspired life. This book is a guide to living that life.

As a psychiatrist, I have devoted myself to understanding the essence of healing and the ways we as human beings can live to our fullest potential, content in our lives. I have learned many modalities for treatment and therapy. Although all have some efficacy, very few have a deep, long-lasting impact. All have some value and may improve the quality of life for certain people, but too often the traditional approaches tend to be too superficial, the solutions reductionist or materialistic. And so the problems recur.

I have been privileged to learn from many teachers, but it is Dr. Valerie Hunt who was one of the most influential. Dr. Hunt successfully created a model of the divine human based on the human bioenergy field, which integrates behavior, emotions, the mind, and health. This model has led me to think and work within a new paradigm for psychiatry, one based not on pathology, symptoms, and medications, but rather on the essence and potential of the divine human. I have found that the application of this model in my psychiatric work goes deeper and has a more sustained effect on those who are ready to have the most profound insights and who desire to evolve to a greater level of awareness and expanded consciousness.

Throughout this book, you will notice that I refer to "expanded" self-awareness and "expanded" consciousness and not "higher" consciousness. The reason for this, as you will come to see, is that to be truly open, stable, and whole, we need a full range of awareness. In other words, awareness of the body—everything about being physical and grounded—is every bit as important as being creative, mystical, spiritual, and soulful.

There is a misconception that having self-awareness means being self-referential. When I speak of self-awareness, I do not mean it as self-absorption, self-centeredness, selfishness, or narcissism. There have been some arguments made that we are getting too "me" oriented and losing our ability to experience and feel empathy and compassion. To some extent I would agree, but I believe that when we are living with expanded self-awareness and expanded consciousness, we cannot help becoming even more aware of the world and the people around us in a greater empathic, compassionate, and proactive way. As we accept and love ourselves as a prerequisite to loving unconditionally, we come to accept and love others in a more sustained and sincere way.

This book is divided into three parts: Intuition, The Bioenergy Field, and The Mind-Field: Emotions, Life, Body, and Soul. Each of these parts builds on the one before it and is followed by insight-generating questions, exercises, and guided visualizations/ meditations to help you toward your own expanded self-awareness. In describing the work I do through inspired life psychiatry and in writing this book, my intention is to make these ideas, skills, and possibilities for expanded consciousness and an inspired life available to all.

INTRODUCTION

How I Got to Where I Am

The Twists and Turns Along the Way

We all have a unique story—the one that tells our journey of becoming who we are. In becoming aware of the moments, people, and events in our stories, we begin to define the process of our evolution. Although I hesitate to spend time on my own story, it may serve as an example, a map that lets you see the path—the twists and turns—that I have taken so far. Like a jigsaw puzzle with many pieces that at first don't seem to have a place, as more and more pieces snap together to define the picture, even the oddest-looking pieces fit. Although it is my story, it may encourage you to look at how your life's map has unfolded and to find your own jigsaw pieces. My story may help you to understand how you and I have evolved into who we are through all of life's changes.

No one who knew me as I was growing up would ever have expected that I would become a physician or a psychiatrist. I had always been an artist and an actor, a performer who loved the process and expression of creativity and art in all its forms. Clearly I was more intuitive than scientific. Although I was never discouraged from expressing creativity, I sensed that I needed to maintain the language of intellect to communicate well in my family. At some point I realized that I was "good" with people— that I had a capacity for compassion and empathy. Even without verbal communication from someone, I often could feel what he or she felt, have an insight to, or understand a detail about his or her feelings, life, and struggles. I had a sense of "knowing" about others.

At various points I shed my different artistic commitments. Although I loved dancing—at one point I was highly committed to being in that profession and was already a member of a ballet company—I realized that to pursue it further would mean a life entirely focused on my physical body. So I stopped.

I love art and originally majored in fine art and psychology with the idea of being an art therapist. For a time, the allure of art made me think I would be a commercial artist, but after two years of study, I began to have the same thoughts I had as a ballet dancer: that a life in art would be a very self-focused one. At my core I realized that I would never be fully satisfied in that profession, so I changed my major to psychology and sociology.

When I was almost done, I awakened one day knowing I needed to go to medical school. As the daughter of a doctor who had lived her entire life witnessing the demands and the pros and cons of medicine, being one myself had been the furthest thing from my mind. But that day I knew with unwavering certainty that medical school was the right place for me. It is an understatement to say that anyone who knew me was surprised, and some had little faith that I could do it. But I diligently launched into the premed course of study in spite of not having studied or taken a science course since high school. I experienced a great opening in my mind that I found exhilarating and exciting as I learned to view the world through the lens of the scientist.

I completed my requirements in a year and a half, applied to medical school, and was accepted. I had always been an excellent student, finishing among the top of my class, graduating summa cum laude and Phi Beta Kappa. However, attempting medical school with such a rudimentary knowledge of science and the minimum premed requirements presented great academic challenges and was intellectually a most humbling experience. In spite of consistently being in the bottom of the class the first two years, I loved every aspect of medicine. Every specialty I studied was one I could imagine pursuing. But in the end, psychiatry—with its promise of the unexplored frontier of the brain, the psyche, emotions, behavior, and relationships—won out.

I embarked on my residency, and in Harry Wilmer, MD, I found my first true mentor. He was a Jungian psychiatrist with an extraordinarily keen mind, a scientist, a brilliant therapist, and a highly intuitive man—a person ahead of his time, and in short, a perfect role model. I finished my residency, did a year of specialty as a fellow in child psychiatry, worked for the state mental health department as an adult and child psychiatrist, and followed that up by starting a private practice. Later I also worked part time as the medical director/psychiatric consultant for the San Antonio Rape Crisis Center.

For years I was on a schedule, one that dictated what time I got up and when I went to work. Work was defined in perfectly measured increments of fifteen, thirty, or sixty minutes, one person at a time. As a psychiatrist I empathically listened with my ears, my heart, and my mind. I listened so hard to what was said and not said that when I developed tinnitus and the doctor said, "You have hyper hearing," I laughed. The metaphor was there, blatantly staring at me—the strain of listening so intently had manifested as constant ringing.

I tried numerous treatments: medications that made me sleep, gain weight, lose weight, pee. I tried herbs, homeopathy, meditation, insight, craniosacral therapy, adjustments, Oriental medicine, and energy manipulation. Nothing changed the shrill, high-pitched ringing that reminded me interminably of how much I had heard, of how hard I had tried to hear, and of what I was not hearing.

My preoccupation with tinnitus was a marker telling me I had reached a point of overload and burnout. I had spent time trying to listen—it was my job, after all. But there was much I was not hearing, not only from others, but myself as well.

I reached a point of dreading hearing anyone's story. Wherever I went, I tried to steer clear of people. What a change for this person whose whole life had revolved around the idea of helping others! I, who had always been someone who listened to another's life story, often random and unsolicited such as on an airplane or while waiting in a line, now became a person who put on headphones to avoid listening.

Tinnitus has been a persistent symptom, even to this day, but as I have searched for resolution it has led to me to ever deeper and greater levels of understanding, insights, and awareness about myself. In the process, I have become less concerned about getting rid of tinnitus and have been grateful that that particular symptom acted as a catalyst to get me to where I am now. If we are paying attention to the meaningful coincidences—also known as synchronicity, as we will discuss later—around us, we are usually led to what is needed for our next level of evolution. My next level of evolution occurred around my forty-fourth birthday.

I had always known I was intuitive, maybe even a little psychic, drawn to all things metaphysical, but I had spent a great deal of energy ignoring it. In fact, I felt as though my artistic/intuitive self and my scientific/rational self played a constant tug-of-war. Hard as I tried, they never seemed to be able to live in peaceful coexistence. A well-known medium in my tai chi class had once told me: "Your soul knows, but your brain gets in the way. It's like you keep picking it up and putting it down again." How right she was!

Forty-Four

> *The number four is a symbol for the orderly arrangement of that which is separate.*
>
> —J. E. Cirlot[1]

As an ardent student of Carl Jung's analytical psychology, I sensed an auspiciousness to my forty-fourth birthday. The number four was given prominence in its symbolism by Jung and even earlier in history. Although the symbolic meaning can be obtuse, convoluted, and complex, in essence Jung saw it as a stabilizing number and therefore strongly linked with individuation.[2] Individuation is the process through which an individual, as a result of personality, psyche, and life's experiences, develops into a unique person who is becoming integrated into a whole being. It is a stage in the development of consciousness. I think of my forty-fourth year as the time when my transformation into a more integrated, conscious, self-aware person really began. I can mark the beginning of this transformation to a specific time, place, and occasion—a birthday celebration for an acquaintance. That is where I first met June.

June and I bonded instantly. Although we were five years apart in age, our lives had been on parallel tracks. Both of us had been born Jewish and had gone to the same temple yet were more inclined toward nonreligious spiritual ideas. We both had a favorite teacher, Mr. Bendiner, an ethics teacher of sorts, an old, complicated, wise curmudgeon of a man whom most students tried to avoid. June and I had been in the same high school, same social and youth clubs, even the same ballet company. We had gone to the same university, June starting as a science/premed student but ending up in art, and I having started as an art student but ending up in premed. Of course there were some differences, but those unfolded over time and were not as important in that first meeting, which was made significant by the commonalities we shared.

The coincidence was enough for me to ask my newfound friend, who worked as a massage therapist and bodyworker, if she could help with hip pain that I had begun to experience. June responded that she could work on me but also suggested I see a chiropractor who worked in "unusual, nontraditional ways."

In this chiropractor I felt I had found a brother. He was well grounded in traditional chiropractic manipulations but open to alternative methods of working with the mind-body connection. As I read and studied his textbooks, I learned kinesiology—the study of muscle mechanics—along with learning about meridians, the energy pathways identified in Oriental medicine that are used in acupuncture (think of these as the energy version of the circulatory or lymphatic systems), and other energy systems (we will discuss the energy centers or chakras in Part II). A whole new world opened to me, one I sensed I had been waiting for.

What was happening, I believe, is best explained by one of my favorite quotes from W. H. Murray, who describes beautifully the process I was entering:

"Until one is committed, there is hesitancy, the chance to draw back. Concerning all acts of initiative (and creation), there is one elementary truth, the ignorance of which kills countless ideas and splendid plans: that the moment one definitely commits oneself, then Providence moves too. All sorts of things occur to help one that would never otherwise have occurred. A whole stream of events issues from the decision, raising in one's favor all manner of unforeseen incidents and meetings and material assistance, which no man could have dreamed would have come his way. Whatever you can do, or dream you can do, begin it. Boldness has genius, power, and magic in it. Begin it now."[3]

Jung is known, among other things, for defining the concept of *synchronicity*.[4] Synchronicity is the simultaneous occurrence of events that appear significantly related but have no discernible causal connection—what we commonly call coincidence. Synchronicity might take the form of an event or chance meeting that leads to another, then another. Even if we miss some of the messages, they are often repeated until we become attentive to the guidance the synchronistic events are trying to give us. If we are lucky and aware and are willing to accept the guidance— the meaning and the mystery—we may end up with new relationships, new learning, and new insights. Paying attention to these "coincidental" experiences and what they might mean can lead to a wiser, more expanded state of consciousness.

Like everyone else, I have had many of these moments. Some I have eagerly snatched up and many I have missed. Fortunately, both my own inner compass, which has never relented in guiding me through understanding symbols and metaphors, and the persistence of "Providence" allowed me to pay enough attention to continue on a steady course toward evolving consciousness.

Synchronicity continued to cross my path. Realizing that I was open to ideas related to energy being an important and integral component to our body and mind, the chiropractor recommended a workshop. I was hesitant; the facilitator called herself a psychic, and the course was called Illume-a-Nation.[5] But guided by that inner radar called intuition, I knew where I needed to be. In the course that weekend, I learned how to muscle test using kinesiology and how to "speak" to and access unconscious information by using the body. The information I accessed was related to limitations and blocks created by belief systems.

(Subconscious and unconscious are often used interchangeably.

Subconscious is information that will surface when we focus on it. Unconscious is a term that was coined by Freud and refers to the deeper information, repressed thoughts, memories, or beliefs that are not as easily remembered. We can think of it like this: subconscious is like a mole on the side of your thigh that you are not likely to notice it unless you look down, see it, and note its presence; unconscious is like a mole on your back—you will not see it at all unless you make an effort to do so by holding up a mirror or unless someone else points it out to you. Kinesiology was a useful vehicle for getting to that level of unconscious information.

In the midst of the standard "new age" psychic jargon, I noticed a shift occurring within me, subtle yet noticeable. Even my family noticed a difference after the workshop. The workshop had shifted my perceptions about many of my own belief systems and uncovered emotional blocks I didn't know I had. For example, I discovered I had numerous blocks related to being a woman and a professional at the same time.

The changes I noted in myself and others at the workshop were enough to motivate me to become a diligent student and an ardent, objective observer of myself. With myself as guinea pig, I set out to systematically test my experience.

As I learned at Illume-a-Nation, kinesiology is the primary yet limited form of communicating between the unconscious and the tester. This communication occurs through using the body as the conduit and liaison. Kinesiology is limited in that it is only a "yes/no" system of communication. The yes/no answer depends on muscle strength when any muscle is forced to resist pressure on it. Strong, unyielding muscles indicate a yes response while weak, collapsing ones are no. (In the appendix, I include information on this method and basic instructions on using kinesiology.)

Using the methodical, structured template I had learned from the psychic, I employed questions selectively formulated to identify unconscious blocks or "limiting decisions." I thought of these blocks as inner programming. I diligently kept a journal while employing the method I had learned and soon saw patterns emerging, shifts in the way I perceived and reacted to certain situations, and clarity about what was happening. This allowed me to create a less obtuse—less "new agey"—vocabulary to describe the process. This method, though lacking the depth that I later developed, was my first conscious and systematic exploration of the mind-body-soul connection.

Many of my beliefs and attitudes were changing, including becoming more open about my trust in this "stuff" and in my own intuitive capacity. I dared to talk about kinesiology in the staff meetings of my office group and confessed to my once-a-month lunch colleagues what I was doing. I went so far as to demonstrate kinesiology to anyone who asked (and sometimes to those who didn't). For the first time, I was not concerned about what others might think. Surprisingly, many of my colleagues were receptive, curious, and open. (There were also some who were not. I later heard that one of my colleagues at that time said, "Helen has gone off the deep end!")

It is remarkable that when the universal consciousness (also recognized as destiny, God, the greater intelligence, or spiritual guides) wants to get our attention, dramatic events occur. The first occurred when I was faced with the possibility of using the kinesiology method with my patients. I suggested that Pam, a patient I had just started seeing in therapy, attend the Illume-a-Nation workshop. I was going to be there as a facilitator in training. Pam had come to me with a history that suggested she would be in therapy for a very long time. She needed several medications to control her symptoms of depression and anxiety. In the first day of the workshop, she had a profound experience that seemed to resolve many of her issues and symptoms in one fell swoop.

Pam came into our next therapy session looking like a different person, saying that her coworkers had noticed the change in her and asked her where she had been because she looked so relaxed and happy. She told them she had been on a retreat. The changes in her were so obvious that they all said they wanted to go on that retreat! Pam soon felt comfortable discontinuing all her medications, and only a few sessions were needed to process her profound experience. I saw her periodically in the outside world, and she always described constancy in the transformation she had experienced. Only once did she return for more therapy. By that time, I was doing something quite different in addition to kinesiology—but more on that later.

Even more dramatic was an event with another patient. Gina had been seeing me for a long time and was being treated with a combination of therapy and medications. The diagnosis was uncertain, but Gina often dissociated, expressing herself as if she were a child or teenager. As the mother of several young children, she would buy dollhouses and toys for herself, hiding them and not wanting to give them to her daughters. She was resistant to becoming independent, continuing to accept help from her parents following a painful divorce even though she had a profession that she chose not to practice. Realizing she needed to get a job, Gina went into a period of decline. She became anorexic and was on the verge of needing hospitalization. The worst moment occurred when she huddled into a fetal position on the floor in the corner of my office, tearful and uncommunicative. Not knowing what else to do, I muscle tested for blocks related to the issues of independence and the fears that accompanied them.

After going through the method, including a guided meditation for transformation that acts as the energetic vehicle for assisting with resolving the blocked decisions, she was relaxed, present, and clear thinking. The following week she returned and told me that she had been reading an article on massage therapy while in the waiting room and thought she might like that. Within a few weeks, she registered for massage therapy school and received certification. She began a massage therapy practice, and after steady improvement, she eventually decided that she could return to her profession.

When I asked what she thought had made the difference that enabled her to go back to work, she replied that the kinesiology work we had done had been a significant component. I agreed. That was the only thing we had done differently. From then on Gina seemed to need fewer sessions and less medication. She stopped dissociating almost completely, and subsequently faced her adult challenges with a serious commitment to her therapy and with increasing appropriate behavior. She now only comes in for medication checks every four months, and longer sessions only in infrequent times of crisis.

I restructured the format of the Illume-a-Nation course and, with the originator's permission and blessings, created my own version of the method. I called it "Psy-Ki" and taught it in workshops to professionals, therapists, nurses, and lay people. My hope had been that they would continue to use the method on their own in order to continue identifying limiting blocks, clearing them, and making changes. Although everyone who learned the method liked it, very few people continued to use it after the workshops.

In my eagerness to share what I thought was a valuable tool toward healing, I explained and demonstrated the method wherever I went. At conferences, especially at the National Institute for Clinical and Applied Behavioral Medicine (NICABM) conference I attended in 1998 (I will share more on the significance of this particular conference to my process later in the chapter), I found myself giving mini workshops over breakfast, in the hallways, and late at night. People wanted me to explain, teach, and demonstrate. It was so easy to learn and could be so effective that I did not want to hold back on disseminating the information.

Muscle testing always seemed to reach quickly into the deep recesses of the unconscious and confront the most salient issues; the result was an immediate response to the demonstration. A well-known self-help author and conference presenter became fascinated by my unusual method when we talked about it. I demonstrated the method on her and she saw the immediate results. Since she was on the board of NICABM, she encouraged me to send in a workshop proposal for the next conference.

I submitted a proposal and did not hear back from them. Although I felt somewhat discouraged, I chose to pay attention to the synchronicity and wondered whether in being rejected, I needed to follow a different path. My path became one that would take me much deeper and to much more profound levels of awareness. Had I been accepted as a presenter, I would have most likely stayed with my method and possibly would not have evolved further. To do so, I had to go beyond and relinquish my focus on teaching Psy-Ki.

NICABM and Valerie Hunt

The National Institute for Clinical and Applied Behavioral Medicine (NICABM) held an annual conference entitled Psychology, Immunology, and Consciousness in La Jolla, California. Every year I received the brochure but had never attended. But in 1998, it was as if neon lights lit up the registration form, and I knew that I needed to go. I selected which workshops I would attend, registering for all the sessions that related to my use of kinesiology for accessing unconscious blocks. The real enticement to attend was Ilana Rubenfeld, a therapist who used bodywork as a way to attain psychological information.

A few months later, I arrived in La Jolla. I was confident of why I was there and what I was there to learn. The first evening I found myself with a group of conference attendees waiting for a table at the hotel restaurant. We all decided to sit together. Getting to know each other, I turned to the woman sitting next to me and asked what she had come to the conference to learn. Without hesitation she answered, "I want to know more about intuition." Intrigued by this response, I asked her how she had decided which courses to attend. She responded that she had used a pendulum. I asked her to show me how she did it, and she pulled out a pendulum and demonstrated yes and no responses. Stunned, I realized that the pendulum with its yes/no response was similar to kinesiology.

I went to my room and decided to test to see which of the numerous sessions offered would test strong. Since each hour of this weeklong conference was filled with multiple options for workshops and sessions, all of which were numbered followed by their title, I could fold the pages of the catalogue to cover the titles of the workshops and "blindly" move my finger down, testing each session number without seeing or knowing what the content was. I tested the numbers to see which would test yes. I fully expected to see a pattern that would follow the choices I had already made, but that was not what happened. All the yes answers were for the courses and classes on intuition. None of the ones I had already chosen was a yes.

I felt as if I had been punched in the gut. In the ongoing dispute between my psychic/artistic/mystical self and my rational/scientific/logical self, intuition was caught in the middle. I decided to trust the testing, and I changed all the sessions I had originally signed up for to the ones on intuition.

Having done that, I left my room and wandered around the book displays being set up. I was drawn to a table with books and CDs by an author named Valerie Hunt. Although there were many books and recordings, two titles caught my attention: a set of CDs called *Music of Light* and a book titled *Mind Mastery Meditations*. Valerie Hunt's student, who was setting up the table, told me that there would be a longer major workshop related to that book. After talking together for a while, the student assured me that Valerie would want to speak with me, so I waited.

When Valerie came, her vitality and vivaciousness surprised me. Dressed in bright turquoise and wearing large colorful earrings, this eighty-three-year-old woman gave the impression of a much younger one. As she began to talk, the vibrancy and clarity in Valerie's eyes convinced me that she was a valuable teacher and a person who could provide the guidance I was seeking. I explained how I used kinesiology to tap into unconscious information. Valerie told me that kinesiology was too superficial. At the time I bristled, but I filed the comment away.

We talked for two hours. We talked through the next keynote speaker's presentation and stopped only when it was time for Valerie's book signing. I bought the *Music of Light* CDs. These have become a focal point and anchor for me personally and in my work. In brief, the music—classical, new age, etc.—included sound frequencies produced by specific color spectrums emanating from the energy of the body. Each frequency had a specific effect—calming, energizing, and so on—depending on the color frequency of a specific energy center in the body. When I returned home I played it for my young son. Because he loved listening to it and it soothed him, the lavender, relaxing spectrum became an occasional component of his bedtime ritual.

Valerie and I talked until it was time for the following keynote speaker. She suggested I attend her workshop. I was still on the fence. She got up to leave, as did I. When I walked into the large auditorium and the keynote speaker was introduced, I was surprised to see that it was Valerie Hunt! I was starting to have the feeling that I needed Valerie's workshop and that it was probably the reason I had come to this conference.

After the lecture, the student I had met earlier muscle tested me to see if I would test strong or weak for attending Valerie's workshop. I tested strong. Having committed to trusting my responses and my intuition, I went to make the change in workshop choices. There was only one space left for Dr. Hunt's workshop, and even though it meant not participating in Ilana Rubenfeld's major workshop, I took it.

Dr. Hunt's workshop proved an important milestone. I learned the basics and understood the tools for opening and getting information from the "mind-field," Dr. Hunt's term for what I then equated with the unconscious. In the course of the workshop and the exercises, I had a profound enough experience—as did most of the people who filled the ballroom to overflowing—to convince me of the validity of Valerie's theories and method. Even though my ever-skeptical side tried to argue against it, I resonated with Valerie's concepts of "lifehoods," or past lives, which I will discuss in depth in Chapter 17.

Home from NICABM after learning Valerie's way of working with the mind and mind-field, I engaged a number of patients and myself in the work. The experiences were always deeply moving and profound for both my patients and me. Pam, who had been my validating experience in the kinesiology work, returned. She had been having disturbing heart palpitations, and before she launched into intensive medical evaluations and treatments, she had sought me out to see if there might be a different way to make sense of these symptoms.

Fresh with the passionate resonance of Valerie's work, I suggested a mind-field session. Pam lay on the table. I guided her in the process of calibrating her field and instructed her to visualize a blank screen. She began to get anxious but stayed with the process. Images began to emerge, which she described to me: a child, a dress, a garden. Using the technique learned from Valerie, I kept supporting Pam in the emerging images, guiding her into increasing clarity about what she was "seeing." The snapshots that came up eventually aligned into a coherent experience—an antebellum lifehood, or past life. Pam eventually described a traumatic event that led her to experience deep and profound emotion. The experience made perfect sense to Pam. She had a release and a sense of resolution after the session. I didn't hear from her again but ran into her several years later. She was very content and reported that after that session she no longer experienced palpitations. This dramatic result attracted and held my attention.

Despite this success and others, after two years, I felt increasingly stagnant. I stopped using mind-field work, opting for EMDR (eye movement desensitization and reprocessing), a technique specific to treating post-traumatic stress disorder (PTSD). EMDR is less abstract and less focused on deeper soul searching, so it felt less demanding than delving into the mind-field. It is a proscribed protocol that was not complex to learn or use. The theory is founded on the establishment of new neural networks rather than the understanding of the subtle underlying energetics of the process. I studied it, became certified, and used it in my work with patients who had trauma and PTSD.

In retrospect I realize EMDR was attractive to me because it had a stronger community of practitioners and did not require working on my own inner state. This made the technique more comfortable to use than Valerie Hunt's work, which had very few other practitioners and demanded self-exploration and insight. However, after using EMDR for a while, it became clear to me that neither the EMDR community, NICABM, nor any other professional venue was offering whatever it was I needed to get unstuck and progress.

The stagnation I experienced was not just in my profession but also personally. My son's emerging turmoil as he entered adolescence triggered my own. The challenges of parenthood became increasingly difficult to negotiate. I knew my own sense of disorientation could not be helping our son's struggle to gain his bearings. In desperation, four years after meeting her, I contacted Valerie Hunt. She agreed to speak with me, something she apparently was not doing with others. In that conversation, she informed me that her focus was now on large groups globally and not on individuals. Although she was not able to work with me, she gave me the name of someone who could. Her name was Suzanne Lahl, and she lived in Hawaii.

Suzanne had met Valerie at the same conference I had. After the conference she had suspended what she had been doing in her field of organizational development and went to work with Valerie. Now, while Valerie took on the world, Suzanne did mind-field work with individuals. All the stars must have been aligned, because at the time I started working with Suzanne by phone, she was planning a workshop in Denver within the next few months. It was much easier to get to Denver than to Hawaii, so, without hesitation, I signed up. Thus began my intense work with Suzanne, which lasted for the next five years. This groundwork prepared me for the pivotal work I would do with Valerie Hunt later on.

During my time with Suzanne, I gained several insights. My first insight was that I had not wanted to face the depth of emotions associated with my son's moving into his own life, apart from ours as a family. As pleased and proud as I was of him, I couldn't help but feel some sadness and loss—and shame. I had loved the experiences we had shared while he was growing up and was reluctant to no longer have them. There was an inner tension: I did not want to hold my son back or keep him dependent as a child, but I could not help feeling that there was something deep and maybe even archetypal in what I was going through. I recognized it was time to understand what I was feeling and do mind-field work on this issue.

The second insight came when I realized my turmoil was not about my son at all but about my fears of not being stimulated or challenged, or feeling the passion that I had experienced as a mother. The third insight was that I was afraid of and did not know how to effectively express emotions. The fourth, the greatest, was that I was afraid of not manifesting my full capacity or tapping into my well of creativity—in other words, I was afraid of not living a meaningful life.

Uncovering beliefs I had about myself, especially about myself as a woman and an intuitive, and taking responsibility for being a powerful person was a difficult and emotional process. I approached it as the most important journey and research of my life and faced it head on, never flinching or letting myself off the hook. I knew that the process of identifying the erroneous belief systems and taking full responsibility for who I wanted to be was a matter of becoming aware of ever-deeper levels of consciousness by accessing the mind-field.

The experience I had with the mind-field work changed me in the deepest and most profound ways I had ever experienced. It seemed to get at the core of my psyche in a way Psy-Ki had not. Psy-Ki was inherently vague and lacked depth. Even though there was a *sense* of transformation, it occurred in a mysterious, obscure manner, lacking the deeper self-awareness that comes from experiencing, understanding, owning, and taking responsibility for the process. In short, it was what Valerie had called it—too superficial.

With mind-field work I noticed that my awareness and thinking were clearer and sharper. Belief systems that had held me back all my life were blown out of the water. The confusion with numbers, directions, and sometimes words that I had always experienced (which I realized later was mild dyslexia) improved considerably. My sessions with Suzanne were always nontraditional, unusual, and challenging but deeply moving. Spontaneously, I experienced intense emotions brought on by what I was seeing in my mind—experiences that did not correlate, even metaphorically, to the experiences of my life. What I was seeing were images of what I identified as myself but in times and places other than this life.

I had always been a good daydreamer, and I could fantasize like a champ, but never before in daydreaming or fantasy had I experienced such a depth of emotions. Nothing that was not "real" had ever elicited this response, no matter how moving the book, the movie, or the art. The intensity of emotions was unique—always followed by a sense of resolution completion and an unquestionable sense of ownership of the experience, with a connectedness to something greater. I observed myself changing in my relationships to others and, more important, to myself.

It might have been irrational or impossible to prove, but I had to consider that I was experiencing reincarnation memories, and that in identifying and releasing stuck emotions, I was undergoing an indisputable transformation that felt like a deep resolution. Although I could not understand it fully, it felt true. The next step for me, therefore, was to understand reincarnation, its implications, and how it related to what was happening to me to the fullest extent that was humanly possible. What I have come to understand about reincarnation is something that I will write more about in the final part of this book.

Mind-field work meant I was working within the realm of higher consciousness, and with that came the recognition that bioenergy—the field from and around the body that is pure energy—played a significant role. It was during this time that I became a student of tai chi, a form of martial art that relies on generating internal energy and harnessing its power. I soon experienced and could feel this energy moving internally and externally. While engaged in the practice, I could sense vibrations, tingling, and heat, sensations that were intensified the more focused I was. This reinforced the idea that once we become attuned to subtle energy, we begin to develop enhanced sensitivity to psi phenomenon, including intuitive information, prescience, telepathy, clairvoyance, and other paranormal occurrences.

As an example, I had a friend who became gravely ill after surgery to treat a chronic disease had required inducing a semi-comatose state. He did not appear to be responding well to the treatment. Unable to communicate in any other way, I connected with him mind to mind. I "saw" him on the fence, undecided if he would live or die. I "talked" with him and challenged his choice to die because he was tired of the medical complications, forgetting the rich and loving life he had. I enlisted the help of his wife and daughter. Being the remarkable person that he is, he chose to live and, against all odds, began to improve. He was able to tell me what he remembered while in this comatose state, validating all the images I had "seen," including his being on the fence and the conversation we had. As he began to recover, I brought June in to work with him. As a result of her energy work, he improved significantly, and with her help and the firm foundation of the love of his wife and daughter, he recuperated fully.

Witnessing my friend's recovery through energy work and the validation of my nonverbal communication with him piqued my interest in the healing of the body through the power of the mind and energy. I learned from June that the energy work she used was a combination of many energy modalities, including Reiki. To learn most modalities would require a level of commitment I could not make, but Reiki was something I could learn relatively quickly.

I found a class with a local teacher, and, as expediently as possible, I went through the training. (Many years later I repeated the training with Brian Dailey, M.D. from New York, who helped enhance my skills greatly). I discovered that when I placed my hands on people, I would instantly connect with their mind-fields and could feel or see their emotions and the experiences or situations affecting their physical conditions. This was most profound with the patients and families I worked with when I volunteered at the Cancer Therapy and Research Center.

As I realized with excitement how my intuition and increasing perception of energy and the mind were coming together, I discussed my experiences with my Reiki instructor and fellow practitioners. My instructor asked me to put together a class on how to use intuition with Reiki. Although I had taught several workshops on intuition, I decided to approach it differently, from the perspective of the mind-field, and prepared the workshop as a way to clarify my own thinking on the ideas that were emerging.

It was all coming together: the energy work, the intuition class, the kinesiology class, and my evolving understanding of the mind-field. What had begun as one course on intuition and Reiki evolved into a two-part bioenergy course with the promise of a third. It took years of learning, observing, processing, consolidating, and evolving, but I was ready to take full ownership of my knowledge and the manifestation of it. Realizing, however, that my work was founded on Valerie Hunt's model, I decided it was time to visit her once again. I telephoned and made an appointment for what she then called a life-shock session, but my real intent in calling her was simply to connect with her. Her standard session was three hours, and that is all I expected.

When I got to Valerie's home in Malibu, we talked for many hours, essentially picking up where we had left off a little over ten years before. There was a strong and powerful connection. I had finally reached a level of mastery where we could meet not only as teacher-student but also as colleagues and friends. The three hours became three days. At some point she asked if I would collaborate with her as the psychiatrist for work on research she was planning to do. I readily accepted and began my most important personal and professional work.

Traveling to California frequently to work directly with

Valerie and speaking with her over the phone on a regular basis, I gained a much deeper, scholarly, and profound understanding of bioenergy fields, the mind-field, emotions, behavior, health, and the human psyche. She wanted all those who collaborated with her to engage in their own self-exploration; these people included engineers, oncologists, and even potential financial backers. I, pleased to have an opportunity to work so closely with her, continued with mind-field/life-shock sessions along with our in-depth discussions. My personal work in these life-shock sessions allowed me to become a partner to Dr. Hunt and to evolve into a new way of thinking about psychiatry. As I completed developing Part I and Part II of the bioenergy course and began to develop Part III, I realized that the course I was preparing was not only about intuition and bioenergy, but also how these play a role in our healing and evolving consciousness. It was, in fact, a course for expanded self-awareness—for how to live an inspired life.

Inspired Life Psychiatry

Living Aware and Inspired is a newer reiteration of the first self-published version (*Expand Your Awareness, Inspire Your Life*) of what I learned and felt compelled to share. It describes the information, concepts, and methods of the inspired life and what I call INSPIRED Life Psychiatry. This book encompasses everything I know up to now that can lead to a life of clarity, capacity, enjoyment, and meaning.

INSPIRED is an acronym holding within it the components needed to live an inspired life with expanded self-awareness. We need *Intuition* to hear the subtle voice of the mind and to know what to do with it. We need the brain and the *Neurological* system to be the interpreter and the arbitrator. We need the *Spiritual* to give our life meaning. We need to have awareness of our *Physical* condition and body and the interrelationship of the body with mind and spirit. We need *Insight* to be able to make transformations. We need *Resolve* to persist in identifying our internal barriers and patterns that keep us from gaining the information in our mind-field, whether from this life or past ones. We need to identify, open up to, feel, and be free to express *Emotions*, which are at the core of what limits us. The D in the acronym stands for three interrelated d's. When we *Discover* this knowledge of our deepest soul, we blossom into the *Divine* humans we are meant to be, allowing us to fulfill our soul's *Destiny.*

There are many ways to get to the same place. There are many languages to express one concept. I do not state nor pretend that this paradigm is the be-all and end-all. It is not for everyone. We are all at different levels of understanding with different attachments to belief systems. I see this process and myself as something fluid, evolving, constantly changing. By the time you read this, I may already be evolving into a new level of awareness and knowledge. We all evolve in our own time, in our own way, making the choices that we perceive as being the best for us at the time.

But there could be some of you who may find yourselves in the stagnant place I inhabited when this work came to me. You are the ones who may resonate with what I have to say. You are the ones who may find the path to your evolution similar to my own. It is for you that I have put in book form the culmination of all my learning up until now, including what my teachers have taught me. You are the reason I have written this book in a way that makes these complex ideas accessible.

This is my hope: that as you go through the information in this book you will be stimulated and inspired. My intention is to offer you a way to understand who you are and why you made the choices you have made—and through that awareness, to make the changes needed for you to live an exciting, creative, robust, full life. In other words, I hope to enable you to live an inspired life in your highest capacity and to fulfill your soul's destiny, and in doing so, to contribute to elevating the consciousness of the world around you.

PART I

INTUITION

When you reach the end of what you should know, you will be at the beginning of what you should sense.

—Kahlil Gibran, Sand and Foam

CHAPTER 1

WHAT IS INTUITION?

You already know what intuition is. If you have ever had a gut feeling, a hunch, a feeling in your bones, an instinct, a premonition, or a "don't know but just knew it" moment, then you have experienced intuition. But you may wonder what intuition has to do with expanded awareness or an inspired life. Like most people, you may believe that intuition is something that only psychics or people with special gifts have access to.

In fact, intuition is something we all possess. Through intuition we hear, understand, and use information that comes to us from our deepest selves. It is the subtle language we use to understand the information in the bioenergy field and the mind. Intuitive information is invaluable and accurate, and it is important to learn to discern it from all the other bits of information constantly entering our awareness through our senses.

I will ask you what I ask my students at the beginning of my classes: Are you intuitive? Do you pay attention to your intuition? Do you trust your intuition? Do you act on your intuitive information? Some answer yes, and some answer no to the question of being intuitive, but when asked if they *trust* their intuition or if they act on it, almost all of my students answer that they don't. Ignoring intuitive input is like ignoring any other sensory input. If you heard a fire alarm, smelled smoke, or saw flames, would you tell yourself it isn't real? Ignoring intuition is no different than ignoring any information from your other senses.

We all are intuitive. We're born with intuition. Whether or not it's developed, it is there to guide and direct us in our lives. It is a natural and valuable ability. But as I said, most of us don't trust our intuition. There is usually a tug-of-war between the rational self and the intuitive self.

Let's say you're driving on the highway and you have an impulse to take the next exit even though there is no rational reason to do so. Are you more likely to talk yourself out of it or to go with it? Most often we talk ourselves out of it. We let our rational self take over only to find ourselves stuck in traffic because something is blocking the road ahead. The feeling to take an earlier exit was based on something we could not see and had no physical evidence for, yet somehow we had information from somewhere about the block ahead. Taking the next exit was a gut feeling, and nothing about it made sense—until a few minutes later when you were stuck in traffic. Taking a different exit may not be significant, but the signals we get, also known as intuitive information, can be for a wide range of experiences. Many of such signals may prove to be significant or beneficial.

My maternal grandfather and grandmother, who were intellectuals and professionals, lived comfortably in Poland prior to World War II and were both highly intuitive. My grandfather demonstrated this by knowing when he and my uncle needed to leave Poland as the Germans began to take over. He arrived home one day and announced it was time to leave. Since the Germans were beginning to arrest the Jewish men, he and my uncle left first. Arrangements were made for my grandmother and mother to obtain false identities in order to escape and join them later.

My grandmother's intuition guided her when, after several failed attempts to leave, she knew that the next time they *had* to succeed. On the next attempt, she and my mother were able to flee Poland. Later they found out that thirty minutes after escaping their home under their assumed identities, the Gestapo came to arrest my grandmother. She and my mother reunited with my grandfather and uncle in Russia. They were able to avoid the war in Poland by living in a rural camp in Russia. In this way, my family survived the Holocaust.[6]

After the war, they became refugees. Intuition, I imagine, contributed to my grandfather's finding a place where they could settle. Traveling through Europe and then South America, they arrived in Mexico with nothing. My grandfather entered a phone booth and called Jewish sounding names picked from a phonebook. Speaking Yiddish, he called until someone understood him. This is how they settled in Mexico. There, and later in San Antonio, my grandmother, who was an artist and also remarkably intuitive, spent the rest of her life creating magnificent, soulful paintings.

With the powerful tool of intuition available to all, what makes some people trust the information and others ignore it, especially when we are all born with the same ability? The answer will come as we explore what intuition is, how to pay attention to it, and how to trust it.

Intuition is the language of our deepest selves and springs from mind-field information. The mind-field holds all the information about who you are. This information is the repository of the sum of all your experiences, emotions, and belief systems. Having access to this information is the most valuable path to self-awareness. Intuition is the means by which you gain access to the mind-field. Intuition guides you to hear and understand the information contained there. Intuition has a quiet and subtle voice appreciated by those who know and trust it.

I love etymology because the origin of words gives insight into not only the meaning of words, but their contexts. According to the *New Oxford English Dictionary*, the word "intuition" comes from the Latin *intueri*: to look at or to look in/within; the Late Latin *intuitio*: the art of contemplating; and late Middle English denoting spiritual insight or immediate spiritual communication.[7] The origin of the word is meaningful in that it allows us to understand that intuition is a highly personal and internal process strongly related to a spiritual, or higher, function.

A useful working definition of intuition is the process of using ambiguous information for reaching an accurate conclusion—in other words, being able to know or sense information without the use of rational input. Intuition is a natural product of our minds and bodies, a sensory modality for gaining information, and a means for navigating through life with more consciousness. Intuition is not something "new agey" (a term remnant from the 70s), esoteric, dependent on external devices, magic, or witchcraft; it is not an answer or solution to all problems. Intuition is indispensable in receiving information internally and externally from the bioenergy field/mind-field. It serves us in giving us direction as we aim for expanded self-awareness.

We can learn to trust intuition by knowing what conditions enhance it, how intuitive information comes in, what it feels like, what it sounds like, how to know the truth of it, and how to follow its guidance. In the next chapters, we will learn more about the science of intuition, what happens in our body when we are getting intuitive information, and how the brain is involved. Intuition is there as a foundation for us to enhance our lives, to make our lives more exciting, creative, robust, and meaningful.

CHAPTER 2

THE BASIC SCIENCE OF INTUITION

Neurology of Intuition

To bring intuition out of the realm of the fuzzy and into a more scientific perspective, we need to understand how biological and physiological processes correlate to intuition. As methods become more sophisticated, there is increasing research being done (and published in reputable scientific journals) to determine these correlates. Intuition is moving from a strictly paranormal, unexplainable phenomenon belonging to the realm of psychics, hippies, and charlatans to a credible, understandable sensory perception belonging to all. As we learn more about quantum physics, waves, and particles, we are learning there is information in the quantum energy field that, when accessed, is what we call intuition. In this chapter, I will cover rudimentary ideas about the neurology of intuition in order to help you develop a foundation for knowing what intuition is and how to use it.

Knowing a little bit about the neuroanatomy and physiology involved in intuition helps us to better understand the process of receiving and acting on intuitive input. In other words, the hardware is as important as the software. We know that certain parts of the brain are good at accomplishing specific tasks. When it comes to intuition, which is a higher function, we need the brain to work in partnership with the subtler psyche and mind. That partnership is how we begin the process of strengthening our intuition. That cooperation is how we gain access to the information that will lead to our evolution and growth.

Let's begin by looking at how the brain is structured. The brain is divided into two parts called hemispheres. One is on the right, the other on the left. They are connected through a fibrous network called the *corpus callosum*. These two hemispheres are themselves divided into four subsections both on the left and right, called lobes. Each lobe has a different function having to do with thinking processes and behavior.

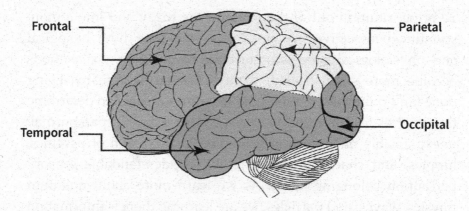

In brief, the *occipital* lobe controls visual processing and recognition of shapes and colors. It tells us how to interpret what we see. The *parietal* lobe is involved in the integration of sensory information that allows for understanding of concepts, as well as goal-directed movement, touch, perception, and recognition of stimuli. It is also involved in sensation, calculation, orientation, language, reading, memory, hearing, smell, speech, behavior, emotions, long-term memory, and intellect; it mediates visual and verbal memory and is involved in reflections upon self and aspects of consciousness. This is where intuitive information may be registered.

The *frontal* lobe is where executive function occurs. It rules, regulates, and inhibits, and is involved in tracking, judgment, movement, personality, reasoning, arousal, and awareness of the environment, our sense of self, and our moral and ethical standards. The *temporal* lobe is important for interpreting what we see and hear, creating memories, and in experiencing, processing, and expressing emotions. It is vital to intuition. Here we interpret what is emotionally important to us. Within the temporal lobe, the hippocampus and amygdala are two structures important to emotions. Since intuition is a way of accessing how we feel, why we feel that way, and what actions we should take, the temporal lobe is significant in the process of intuition. All the lobes may play a part in intuition, but at this time, we have no anatomical location that we can pin down as to where intuition occurs.

For years there have been arguments about the difference between the mind and the brain. Some say the anatomical location of the mind is the brain. But if we see the mind as an aspect of the bioenergy field, and therefore as an information-carrying energy system, then the most interesting aspect of the mind and its functions is that it may not have an anatomical location at all; it is only through the brain that we can make interpretations of that information.

The brain is in constant activity as reflected by electrical charges that we can see as brain wave patterns. The level of activity in these patterns is an indicator of brain behavior. Although there are at least six brain wave frequency patterns that have been identified, not all levels of brain activity are conducive to receiving the subtler information we are exploring. Each wave frequency is differentiated by how frequently they recur in a measurement of time. In the graphs that follow, you will see a range of numbers followed by "Hz." The abbreviation "Hz" refers to a hertz, which is defined as a cycle per second. The lower the number of Hz, the lower the frequency (the waves occur less times per second) of the brain waves, and the higher the number of Hz, the higher the frequency (the waves occur more times per second). The brain wave patterns and the behaviors that correlate with them are as follows:

- *Beta* waves occur during normal waking consciousness, heightened states of alertness, logical processes, times of focused concentration, and while engaging in critical reasoning.

- *Alpha* waves occur during visualization and light meditation, during deep relaxation when eyes are closed, and while daydreaming.

- *Theta* waves occur during deep meditation and dreaming sleep (REM). Many meditators cultivate this type of wave to enhance intuition.

- *Delta* waves occur during very deep sleep or very deep meditative states. These, too, are involved in enhanced intuitive perceptions.

- *Gamma* waves, which occur during high levels of meditation and transcendental experiences, are associated with optimal brain functioning, peak experience, and feelings of oneness, compassion, and happiness. Gamma brain waves are associated with a conscious awareness of reality and increased mental abilities. A Gamma wave is a pattern of brain waves associated with perception and consciousness.

- *Lambda* waves are sometimes called Hyper Gamma waves because they have very high frequencies, 100 to 200 Hz. They are a relatively recent discovery, so not much is known about their function or effect, but they may be linked to states of very high consciousness and "super normal" phenomenon.

- *Epsilon* waves occur in states of consciousness that are extremely focused and elevated, such as when very experienced meditators like Tibetan monks or yogis achieve a state of "suspended animation." In these states there is often no perceived heartbeat, respiration, or pulse.

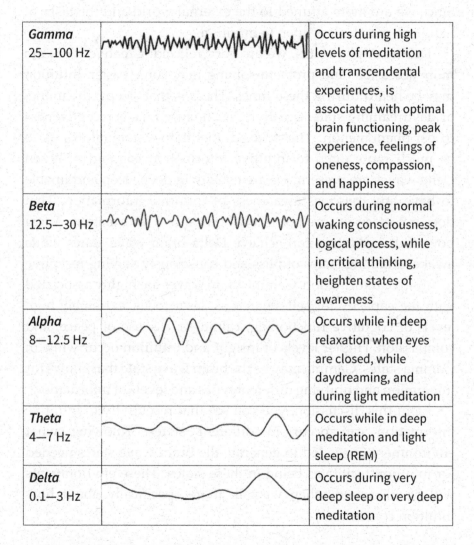

Gamma 25—100 Hz		Occurs during high levels of meditation and transcendental experiences, is associated with optimal brain functioning, peak experience, feelings of oneness, compassion, and happiness
Beta 12.5—30 Hz		Occurs during normal waking consciousness, logical process, while in critical thinking, heighten states of awareness
Alpha 8—12.5 Hz		Occurs while in deep relaxation when eyes are closed, while daydreaming, and during light meditation
Theta 4—7 Hz		Occurs while in deep meditation and light sleep (REM)
Delta 0.1—3 Hz		Occurs during very deep sleep or very deep meditation

Your receptiveness of intuitive information varies depending on your brain wave state. When Beta waves are present and we are in a wakeful state, we are normally the least receptive to intuitive information. In this wakeful state, we are processing information that comes in through our more rational filters—our physical senses. Beta states are energetic, quick thinking, and focused. Since we are more attuned to the external world and the tasks at hand, we may be less open to intuition.

During Alpha states, we are very relaxed. Creative ideas are more accessible and problem-solving may come easier. Intuition may be heard during these times. Theta is that sleepy, dreaming, or daydreaming state. Creativity is enhanced, as is receptiveness to psi phenomenon. This relaxed, meditative state allows us to be much more open to intuitive information coming in. When Delta waves are present, we are usually in deep sleep and unable to have any *conscious* awareness of intuitive information. That does not mean we are not receiving intuitive information. A few powerful meditators can achieve Delta brain wave states while awake, attaining states of bliss and consciously staying receptive to intuitive information. Gamma brain waves are highly associated with the capacity for self-awareness, laser focus, extremely high levels of cognitive functioning, calmness, a sense of peace, and compassion. Higher levels of insight and intuition occur while in Gamma states. Gamma may be the brain wave state that allows for integration and unifying different types and levels of information.[8]

From this discussion, you can see that receptivity to intuitive information can occur in different states. Knowing what environment is needed to generate the brain wave states needed for intuition facilitates being in these states. These environments will be discussed when we talk more specifically about how intuition comes in.

The Yin-Yang of the Brain

If you look at the brain, you will see a large division between the two sides. This split has led to speculation about the respective functions of the left and right hemispheres. The differences appear to have an evolutionary purpose. The left side takes in detailed information needed for survival, whereas the right side takes in a broader and more gestalt view. This difference has led to describing clear demarcations in function, but in reality, there is a great deal of interchange.

When we consider intuition, the right brain appears stronger. It makes sense evolutionarily. The left side may be interested in finding food, making sure that you have the needed tools to get it, and knowing what path to follow to find it. But the left side will need the right side to glean subtle information about the environment and the safety of the area in order to find the food. It may need the right side to sense the presence of the hidden food. This is what we may call *intuitive information* or *nonrational information*. To understand this better, it will be useful to learn the traditionally defined differences between the left and right sides of the brain and how the two hemispheres work together in intuition.

The left brain has been thought of as having logical, analytical, linear, sequential, fact-based, detached, detailed, assertive, and externally focused functions; the right brain has traditionally been thought of as having imaginative, creative, tangential, unordered, intuitive, empathic, holistic, receptive, and internally focused functions.

Left Brain	Right Brain
Logical	Imaginative
Analytical	Creative
Linear	Tangential
Sequential	Unordered
Fact-based	Intuitive
Detached	Empathic
Detailed	Holistic
Assertive	Receptive
Externally focused	Internally focused

But don't be fooled. These seemingly opposing functions are, in fact, a division of labor. The right brain may get the intuitive information, but without the left, it doesn't know what to do with it. In other words, we all need to have confidence in what the right brain is telling us, and we need the support of the left brain to communicate and explain it to others or to know how to act on the information. The left validates the right. Otherwise received intuitive information will have nowhere to go and therefore cannot be helpful in any way.

Take the stereotype of the psychic appearing to have her head in the clouds (who is really just imparting intuitive information from the bioenergy field). Many of us have met one. Generally, these psychics appear to be only right brained. But without the reasoning, analytical, organized part of the brain, they would not be able to communicate anything at all. Or think of an artist who is filled with creative ideas without the organizing skills of the left brain. This artist will not be able to plan to go to the art store to pick a canvas, paints, or brushes. Without the left brain, ideas, creativity, and nonrational information would simply sit in the brain, unable to move, unable to be manifested, and ungrounded. It is important to realize that saying you are a left-brained or right-brained person is not meant to be a part of your identity. Rather, the designation should serve as a signal telling you which side you need to strengthen. Ideally, both need to be strong.

So how do the left and right sides of the brain communicate? Beneath the cortex, between the two hemispheres, the corpus callosum—mentioned briefly at the beginning of this chapter—is a structure composed of numerous wide, flat bundles of neural fibers that connect the left and right cerebral hemispheres. It is through the corpus callosum that the two sides of the hemisphere appear to communicate sensory, motor, and cognitive inform-ation. In the next chapter, we will learn how the corpus callosum affects communication between the left, rational side and the less-rational, intuitive right and how differences in the anatomical structure of the corpus callosum mean differences in how intuition is experienced.

Corpus
Callosum

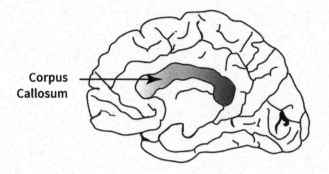

CHAPTER 3

WOMEN'S INTUITION—AND MEN'S TOO

You may be starting to see that although there are clear anatomical sites for many functions within the brain, the higher functions appear to be less specifically located and more interrelated between sites. Things get even more complex and messy if we talk about the differences between men's and women's brains. People generally consider women more intuitive. Even though this is not an entirely accurate idea, there are structural differences in the corpus callosum between men and women that actually may account for these differences.

Men have less dense fibers and fewer connections in the corpus callosum. Their thinking tends to be more compartmentalized, so they are more likely to think of one thing at a time. Men are more reluctant to change. They have more precision in focus and differentiation and are more specialized. Only one issue appears in their radar at a time.

By contrast, women have wider fibers and more connections in the corpus callosum. They are more likely to be able to think about multiple things. They have more connectivity and more willingness to grow and change over time.

Women, in general, are more global, integrated, and integrative, paying less attention to details so that many issues can appear on their radar at the same time (kids, pets, laundry, dinner, world news, and so forth)—a little like keeping a myriad of diverse items in a junk drawer but being able to find that one item that's needed. Women have more access to the right hemisphere more of the time, and with their wider, denser corpus callosum, the communication between left and right brain occurs more seamlessly. Men are more attuned to the left hemisphere, and with the thinner, less dense fibers of the corpus callosum, the communication between the two hemispheres is less readily available.

That is *not* to say men are not intuitive. They are, but they may access intuition differently until they learn to hear the intuitive voice and pay attention to the right brain. Men have intuitive hunches and gut feelings, but because they seem less accessible, these feelings or thoughts are ignored. On the other hand, since a woman has a denser and thicker corpus callosum, which is all about communication between the two hemispheres, she has more *fluidity* in communication between the right and left side.

Because intuitive information comes to the right side, and we know what to do with it thanks to the left, one conclusion we can draw is that if women have greater fluidity in communicating between the left and the right, then women are more likely to have greater *access* to intuitive information and allow it to come in easier. The reason we have the term "women's intuition" may be because of women's greater initial fluidity and access.

Men have less dense fibers and a thinner corpus callosum; therefore, they appear to have less communication between right and left and to be less intuitive. The problem with this conclusion is apparent. How can a visionary like Steve Jobs come up with all those remarkable ideas without intuition? After all, many of his ideas seemed irrational. Another great example is Juan Manuel Fangio, an Argentinean Formula One race-car driver. In the 1951 Monaco Grand Prix, he suddenly slowed down when approaching the bend. He did so completely unaware of why, but this decision allowed him to avoid a multicar pileup that suddenly occurred around the blind corner ahead. This saved his life. He made a decision based on inadequate information—that is, he used his intuition. There are far too many examples of men who are intuitive or act on intuitive information to say that men are not intuitive or even less intuitive than women. In fact, the difference may be said to be quantitative, not qualitative. In other words, men are just as intuitive as women; they just go through a different process to get there.

Mona Lisa Schulz, MD, is a psychiatrist and intuitive who has written brilliantly and extensively on intuition. She describes a wonderful analogy on the difference between men's and women's intuition in her book *Awakening Intuition*.[9] Women's intuition is like an old-fashioned general store, she writes. The classic image of the general store is that of an open space where there is a clutter of items not necessarily well grouped. The brooms might be next to the pickle jars, which are next to the paintbrushes, which are next to the flour, which is next to the buckets—you get the picture. If you call on an old fashioned telephone and ask about a broom and then ask about jars of pickles, the store clerk will be able to manage your questions with just that one call, looking from one place to the other. Men's intuition is more like a well-laid-out department store where all the items are neatly arranged by style, color, or size. If you call in to the suit department and ask about shoes, you will need to call the shoe department instead; if you then want to ask about dress shirts, you have to hang up and call that department. It is more compartmentalized. The end result of both types of stores is that you get what you need; you just get there differently.

Even though men are typically thought of as not being intuitive, it may be that they are not encouraged to be, so they *learn* to ignore their intuition more than women do. Given the chance and the validation, men from all walks of life, ranging from west Texas ranchers to construction workers to vice presidents of corporations, become emotional and awed when their intuition is validated and they are encouraged to own it. When asked if they are intuitive, both men and women tend to answer with uncertainty. The reason for this is that not just men but most *people* are not validated or given the space and the tools to experience the truth of their intuitive information.

In the chaos of our world, things move too fast for us to be still, pay attention, and discern the information coming in. By creating a space that validates the intuitive process, we are all able to discover, hear, and learn to trust our intuitive voice. That space may be found through meditation or mindfulness, or by being in nature. Most of us tend to think of intuitive information as irrelevant or something we are making up. Validating experiences over and over helps give legitimacy to the information we receive and allows us to be more comfortable using intuition and trusting it.

All people—men, women, and children—are excited and relieved when they realize they have the capacity to hear their intuitive voices accurately and to use them. In the next chapter, we'll look at how intuition is developed in children and how it is important to validate that bourgeoning intuition in order for them to learn early on to trust it.

CHAPTER 4

CHILDREN'S INTUITION

All people are born with the capacity to be intuitive. If this is true, what happens to our intuition? Why do some people seem more intuitive than others? It is difficult to research when exactly intuition "begins" because it can be difficult to distinguish between intuition and instinct. In observing children, perhaps even infants, we see clear evidence of them having not just instinctive responses but intuitive ones. Young children are not able to articulate their experience as well as adults, so it is possible that even if they are attuned to the quantum mind-field of information, they cannot tell us about it.

I witnessed my own child having an intuitive experience. When he was quite young, not older than two, we were pulling out of our garage when he suddenly began to scream, "Fire!" He repeated this several times and frantically pointed toward our garage. Clearly there was no fire, and I was surprised he even knew the word. But I was curious, so I took him out of the car and let him lead me to where he was pointing. All the while he continued to scream, "Fire." He pointed high up on a shelf where our camping stove, which he had never seen before, was stored. I calmly told him that yes, this was a stove and that he was right, it did make a fire. With this he settled down, and we continued with what we were doing. Although confirming for him that he had indeed known something about fire seems insignificant, I felt that doing so would let him know that what he had sensed was accurate and not something to be simply dismissed.

I was left impressed by this event. There was no rational explanation; there was nothing related to instinct. He was a very young child who was, to quote our working definition of intuition, "using inadequate information for reaching accurate conclusions," or demonstrating that he was "able to know or sense information without the use of rational input." There are many examples of similar occurrences, and I am sure many parents could relate their own, but because of the limitations of research with children, most of what has been written on this subject remains anecdotal. Still, a great deal can be inferred and gained from observation.

If we postulate that all people are intuitive, probably from birth, then the next question is this: What happens to develop or suppress intuition? I have concluded that there are three discernible factors and experiences that help people develop and hone their intuitive sense in childhood. The first is to come from highly dysfunctional environments, the second is to inherit sensitivity through genetics, and the third is to have received validation of their experience. The second factor is harder to determine since in a family or environment where intuition is a valued ability, being intuitive as a child may appear to be genetic (inherited through biological means) rather than learned (inherited through reinforcement).

Several years ago, as the psychiatrist for the Trauma and Rape Crisis Center, I noticed that people from dysfunctional families seemed to have well-developed intuition. In the setting of the crisis center, where all of the patients were traumatized and/or abused as children, the common denominator was a family of origin that was highly abusive. The patients usually described families in which there was very poor communication and in which emotions were expressed in distorted and inappropriate ways. A young child in this setting acquires the capacity to sense what people are feeling and to gauge the environment—it is a matter of physical, emotional, and spiritual survival. Not only do these children learn to deduce information from the environment and from others, but they also get very good at "attaining direct knowledge or insight without evident rational thought"; in other words, they are good at paying attention to intuitive information.

These patients from abusive families often admit to psi abilities and consider themselves psychic, meaning they have emotional empathy, precognition, clairvoyance, or warnings on death/disaster. However, because of the traumatic overlay, they are usually highly ineffective intuitives. They do not trust or use intuitive information properly. Additionally, many children who are severely traumatized learn to dissociate—they detach themselves from the reality of a difficult physical or emotional experience by not being conscious of it. Since dissociation requires a different state of immediate consciousness, it may open the mind to other levels of sensitivity and awareness. Because of the trauma itself and because they may have been too young, they often cannot be effective in integrating, making sense, or coming to terms with the trauma experience and so become dysfunctional. Nonetheless, with time and greater understanding of the traumatic experience (such as realizing they were not to blame and that the environment in which the trauma occurred was unhealthy and dysfunctional) and through therapy or self-exploration, many of them actually become highly gifted and effective intuitives, psychics, and healers.

A second way children come to know of their intuition is through what we may call genetic means. I have already written about my intuitive grandfather. As an adult I came to realize that my grandmother, an extraordinary artist, my mother, and even my highly intellectual surgeon-father were very intuitive people. Almost before I had even found out I was going to have a baby, my father awakened my mother while vacationing on a remote island near Tahiti to tell her I was pregnant. He would never have called this intuition or even have claimed it as something to notice, but we have come to trust my father's highly intuitive information and often remind him that if he ever "has a feeling" he should buy a lottery ticket, he should buy it immediately! My son, too, appears to have inherited finely tuned intuition.

Still, it is difficult to say whether sensitivity to intuitive information is a biological transmission or an environmental one. As I learn more about energy, I realize that the transmission of intuitive skills may be energetic and not biological per se. I can say that intuition was not overtly encouraged, discussed, or validated in my family. There are many examples of transgenerational psychics, healers, and intuitives, but I cannot determine at this point whether sensitivity to intuition is partially learned, transmitted genetically, energetic, or combinations of all three.

Most of us would like to be enlightened parents, and as such we want our children to have as robust an appreciation of all their senses as possible. We feed our children healthy and interesting foods, take them to the *Nutcracker*, the children's museum, and the farmer's market, knowing that doing so will help them develop an appreciation for different flavors, music, and art. In spite of referring to it as a "sixth sense," too many people think of intuition as a gift rather than a sense, which implies that it is given to only a few and not to others—that it is something precious and extraordinary, not something that is as natural and normal as tasting, hearing, seeing, and smelling.

As I stated before, in the chaos of our world, things move too fast for us to be still or to pay attention and to discern the information coming in. If we create a space that validates the intuitive process, children will be able to discover, hear, and learn to trust their intuitive voices. If we normalize the experience, treating it as natural, children will accept it as just one more skill they can develop and use. I validated and normalized my son's intuition when he yelled "Fire." He is now an intuitive adult. Intuition is a seamless and effortless part of his life, even though he will still say, "I don't know why I suddenly had the feeling I should . . ."

This statement is always followed by something where clearly his intuition guided him.

Intuition is a sense that exists to help us enhance our lives by giving us information from the world all around us in order to protect us, to guide us in making wiser decisions, and to enrich us by allowing greater access to our creativity and levels of understanding. When we succeed in acknowledging it, intuition makes for an awareness that is deep and meaningful—an awareness of our lives, each other, the world, and ourselves. It is worth taking the time and making the effort to cultivate, nurture, and validate this natural ability in children.

CHAPTER 5

HOW INTUITION COMES IN

The Nature of Intuition

We often question what is intuitive and what is not. Intuitive information has several defining characteristics, and once you are aware of them, it is easier to trust that information. Just as the definition of intuition suggests, intuitive information is nonanalytical, neither rational nor logical. However, not every non logical impulse or urge comes from intuition; sometimes urges and nonrational impulses are a reflection of poor judgment or desires and are not to be acted upon. Common sense still has to have a voice—that is, get the left brain in there! An irrational urge to do something endangering or harmful would not be from your intuition.

There are other characteristics to take into consideration. Intuitive information is nonjudgmental, compassionate, and empathic. To be nonjudgmental means that there is no opinion attached to the intuitive information. Compassionate and empathic means the information takes into account concerns for others and for oneself.

There is a misconception that having intuition allows us to be in control of the future or of what happens. In a way, don't we all have that desire? We really want to know how things will turn out. Will that job you've been offered be the best one? Is the person you are dating your one and only? But for information to be truly intuitive, it must be detached from any end result, outcome, or ego. Information does not change according to what you wish to hear or know. To read intuitive information accurately, you need to be willing to give up the control. The desire to control will muddle how you receive intuitive information, just as the difference between seeing through lenses that are clear as opposed to lenses that are scratched up and murky will affect the clarity of what you see.

The final and perhaps most important characteristic of intuition is that it comes in as information accompanied by a sense of certainty, clarity, or knowing. It is experienced as a fact rather than a speculation or wish. You may already be familiar with this phenomenon. Has the phone ever rung and, without looking at caller ID, you knew who it was? Not only that, but you might have just been thinking of that person, perhaps an old college roommate with whom you haven't spoken in a long time. There is no question in your mind who it is. You are certain. There is no "rational" explanation; you simply know. The more experiences you have like this, the more your intuition will be validated.

Clearing the Way for Intuition

Intuitive information can come to you anytime, anywhere; there are no specific requirements for its arrival. Yet to hone your skills, to truly hear the intuitive voice, you need to realize that it is usually a quiet, subtle one. The world in which we live and many of us enjoy—replete with our cable, TVs, smartphones, tablets, and computers—is one with so many distractions vying for our attention that it becomes harder to hear this quiet voice. Increasingly we need to make a deliberate effort to be silent and relaxed and by paying attention to gaps and spaces.

Silence is becoming a difficult state to achieve. When we first considered buying our house, I stepped outside to hear how much traffic was audible. At that time the house was considered almost out of town, which is why we loved it. Surrounded by the edge of the Texas Hill Country with its oaks, cedars, roadrunners, and a magnificent night sky adorned with an abundance of visible stars, we delighted in the quiet, natural environment the property afforded us. Now, thirty-some years later, there are large shopping malls, amusement parks, apartment complexes, and fast-food franchises all around us. Although we still hold on to our oasis where numerous creatures try to find refuge, I can hear a cacophony of cars, trucks, and distant traffic, and the city lights obscure all but the brightest stars.

Our world is not just noisy in auditory ways; our eyes too are assaulted by constant stimulation. When we drive, billboards and advertisements bombard us. We have news channels that inform us day and night, every hour, every minute. They deliver a story, showing us video footage while running a ticker tape underneath with completely different information on it, often with an inserted image of another story, while at the same time advertising what is coming up next and giving us a weather alert. All the while, a panel of newscasters and commentators expound their opinions. Just describing it is exhausting, much less experiencing it!

We have become accustomed to music, TV, and movies wherever we go, wherever we are, whatever we are doing. On a recent trip, I took a break from my iPad and looked out the airplane window. I looked out for a long time, noticing the light, the patterns on the ground below, the clouds. I remembered how I used to travel, sitting at the window seat, deep in reverie, weaving daydreams and visions out of inspirations and ideas, imagining what I could do and *how*. It was a time to be creative and quiet. It's too easy now to play a game, watch a movie, and work, work, work.

I don't think our electronics are a bad thing. But they put us in a position of needing to be more conscious about creating a separate space and time for quiet, reverie, daydreams, imaginings, and creativity. The truth is that most of us like the noise and distractions. Why is that? You probably have thought it would be nice to have some peace and quiet, but you rarely create it. What happens when we are distracted? What are we really distracting ourselves from? Aren't we ultimately distracting ourselves from ourselves, from that very silence, peace, and quiet that we say we want? If we work so hard at distracting ourselves from ourselves, there must be something within us that we are trying to avoid, something we are failing to attend to.

That thing we spend most of our energy trying to avoid is usually our inner knowing, which often comes with associated strong emotions. Although I will speak on emotions in depth in Chapter 14, for now we can say that the emotion we most try to ignore with distraction is fear. Fear loves noise because all that racket keeps the truth of that fear—what it is hiding and what is underneath it—from being seen, from being known. We can pretend we are invincible, infallible, invulnerable, and, yes, immortal, while we play video games, watch reality TV, shop to our heart's content, dance and drink, and take any and all risks as the messages around us suggest we should.

In his wonderful book *Quest for Silence*, Harry Wilmer, MD, tackled this topic brilliantly from a literary, psychological, societal, and cultural point of view.[10] Before he wrote the book, I attended a small Saturday seminar with Dr. Wilmer. A visiting Japanese analyst in the group discussed *ma*, which Harry wrote about extensively later in his book.

The Japanese have a word that captures conceptually and symbolically the importance of the empty space. The word is *ma*, which translates as gap, space, pause, or the space between two structural parts. It implies an interval. To understand the concept of *ma*, you need to know that the structure of silence is gaps and spaces, because when we are silent, we are able to hear, see, and feel the eloquence of the empty space. It is the idea that even an empty vessel is full. *Ma* is not physical; it is experiential. Often it is described as that which gives shape to the whole. Think of our "empty" vessel. A good actor understands this. Watch the greats, and you will notice that the effectiveness of the dialogue in a scene is shaped by the pauses, the silence, the spaces between words.

To demonstrate the importance of silence, read this well-known monologue out loud the way it is written below—no pauses, breaths, or periods.

To be or not to be that is the question whether 'tis nobler in the mind to suffer the slings and arrows of outrageous fortune or to take arms against a sea of troubles and by opposing end them to die to sleep no more.

You should be saying "Huh?" It sounds like a jumbled mess.

Now read it the way Shakespeare wrote it. At the end of each phrase or at punctuations, there is a breath, a pause.

To be, (pause) or not to be, (pause) that is the question: (pause)
Whether 'tis nobler in the mind to suffer
the slings and arrows of outrageous fortune, (pause)
or to take arms against a sea of troubles, (pause)
and by opposing end them: (pause) to die, (pause) to sleep
no more . . .

You can imagine the great Hamlet actors throughout time—John Barrymore, Lawrence Olivier, Richard Burton, Ian McClellan, Jude Law, David Tennant, Jonathan Pryce, and Benedict Cumberbatch—all of whom have been mesmerizing. What is it that makes us catch our breath and feel with the character as we listen to this well-known soliloquy? It is the spaces, the silences, and the pauses that create the drama, engaging us in this archetypal dilemma of being human.

The same concept applies to music. Isaac Stern is attributed to describing music as "that little bit between each note—silences which give the form." These silences are what often suspend us, surprise us, and inspire us in music.

I was so taken with the idea of *ma* that I asked the analyst at Dr. Wilmer's seminar (unfortunately I do not recall his name) to draw the characters related to *ma*—human, time, and space—on a piece of paper. Because this concept of silence in the spaces is not easily understood with our Western vocabulary and we have no correlate in Western ideology for the concept of *ma*, let's examine the character structure and use of the word *ma* in Japanese as shown to me by the analyst.

In Japanese the character 間 is *ma* made up of two elements: *mon*, the outer character meaning gate or door 門, and the inner characters, *hi*, the sun 日, or *tsuki*, the moon 月. This seems to symbolize both the brilliant light (direct) and the reflected light (indirect) that can come through the door when there is silence, and the inner wisdom, information, and intuition that may come into awareness. There are words that have the character *ma* in them. These words incorporate into their meaning the interval between two structures and the experiential nature of it. For example:

人間 *jinkan* — human

時間 *jikan* — time, the initial moment for something

空間 *kuukan* — room, airspace

It is fascinating to me that these important words all incorporate *ma* as if that gap/space/silence is essential to the very fabric of humanness, time, and space. There is a reason I have spent time talking about gaps and spaces and silence. The voice of intuition can be a subtle one, but that quiet voice is how we access the information in the mind. And it is that information that allows us to hear ourselves, to know our truth. In other words, *it is in the silent spaces between thoughts that the innermost self, the truest self, the soul, is heard.*

The time most conducive to hearing the intuitive voice is when we are relaxed. When the body is tensed, it is almost impossible to be in a clear state of mind to receive or hear intuitive information. The exception is in extreme situations, when "something" within us takes over. We might act without much thought, guided by a certainty that this is the correct action. That "something" is probably intuition. To get better at hearing your intuition, you will need to practice creating and getting familiar with the feeling that comes with releasing tension. To do so, you have to create the space for intuition to come in, and the most effective way to do that is by knowing how to relax the body.

I teach a deceptively simple technique for reducing tension in any situation. Try it now. To begin, imagine your body as a "tension meter" that has a range from zero to one hundred. Remember our brain waves? Zero would be extreme relaxation, perhaps comatose and paralyzed; one hundred would be beyond beta, an extreme nonfunctional state or in excessive agitation. The ideal is around thirty to forty, an alert but relaxed state.

The first step is to check in with your body and see where you are in this range. Identify where in your body you are holding the tension, what muscles are tight, where you feel the most physical stress. Take time with this. Most of us admit to holding tension in our necks and shoulders, but you may be holding tension in your fingers, your toes, or even your butt! Find all the places that are holding tension. Then, focusing there, imagine lowering the gauge or the dial by an increment of ten. If you started at seventy, imagine lowering the dial to sixty. Now take it further by imagining yourself going increasingly limp, melting, becoming a rag doll, and lower it by another increment of ten. Keep going until you reach thirty or forty. Notice how different you feel? Is your mind also clearer? This is an ideal state to be in if you want to hear your intuition, because by clearing your body tension, you are shifting the brain waves to more receptive frequencies, and in this way you allow better access to your mind.

Ways Intuition Comes In

Now that we have set the stage for hearing the intuitive voice, we can look at the ways intuition comes in. Intuitive information can enter in many different ways, including through dreams, synchronicity, body sensations, meditation, art, and mental imagery.

Dreams

As a longtime student of Jungian analytical psychology, I find dreams to be of symbolic, mythological, archetypal, and psychological importance. Dreams often reveal what we are unable to know in our consciousness—things that are harder to take in when we are in a conscious state. Sometimes dreams relay information about our weaknesses, warnings, or guidance about something we are not facing in our lives. Sometimes they tell us about our power that we cannot own in consciousness. Have you dreamed about overcoming some evil force or slaying a monster? Sometimes a dream is just a way to get our attention—to make us get a glimpse of what we are capable of or of fears that hold us back. For me, accepting the intuitive information of my dreams came easily and occurred long before I was able consciously to own the power of my intuition and capacity.

Comprehending the language of dreams makes them useful guides, messengers, and psychotherapeutic tools. The language of dreams is rich and complex, often symbolic and metaphoric, and sometimes humorous. One of my favorite dream puns occurred when I was pregnant. My pregnancy was difficult and complicated, requiring bed rest for almost the entire time. Especially at the beginning, there was uncertainty as to whether the baby would make it to term or not. Of course, I was worried and tried my best to stay optimistic while recognizing that my pregnancy might end. It was a profound lesson in being only in the moment. In the midst of this, I had a dream. In this dream my baby was born with a very dramatic nose, a Jimmy Durante nose.[11] (Jimmy Durante was a comic actor famous for an extremely prominent nose.)

In my dream, my baby's nose was even larger and more prominent. I woke up laughing and very sure that my baby would be fine. I could not ignore the pun of my dream. I had been so worried about my baby and his well-being, but this dream was drawing attention to "the baby nose," which I realized was a pun for "the baby *knows*." I knew that meant the baby was fine. He was indeed born fine and with a perfect, cute baby nose!

Example of a dream pun:

Jimmy Durante's nose

The baby "knows"

Synchronicity

Intuitive information also arrives through synchronicity. I introduced you to this term, coined by Carl Jung, when telling my own story. It comes from the Greek words *syn* and *chronos*, which together mean "happening or occurring at the same time" (*syn* means "with," and *chronos* means "time"). Jung used the term to describe the coming together of inner and outer events in a way that is meaningful to the person experiencing it but unexplainable by cause and effect—thus, a meaningful coincidence. If you pay attention, you will begin to notice that there are many examples of synchronicity in your life: a rock in the shape of a heart when you need a comforting message or a hawk flying high when you need strength.

Christine Page, MD, at a workshop on intuition, related a delightful anecdote. She described an exercise where the participants were to think of a problem they were trying to solve or a question to which they needed an answer. Then they were to go outside and find something that resonated as an answer. The participants returned excited by what they found, saw, or experienced that gave them the answers they were seeking.

One person returned disheartened and expressed frustration at having seen nothing. She explained that she was struggling with the question of whether she should take a new job much like the last one she had left, which had been a traumatic one. The only thing she had seen was a neon sign at a shoe repair shop across the street that said "Sole heels while you wait." In reality, the sign—which other people had also seen—said "Soles and heels fixed while you wait," but the lights were out on some of the words and letters. Dr. Page pointed out the synchronistic message in what this person had seen, which was an answer to her question. That message was "*Soul heals* while you wait." The answer to this woman who was about to jump into a new job was that now was not the right time—if she waited, she would have a chance to heal from the last experience.

Another powerful way in which we experience synchronicity is in nature. My office is surrounded by the wildness of the Texas Hill Country. It has four eight-by-eight windows, all facing trees and the outdoors. Often there is a meaningful coincidence that occurs during sessions, frequently related to animals. I was working with a woman who, during this particular session, was struggling with how to deal with an alcoholic husband who would "punch her buttons," so, before she knew it, she would be on the defensive and engaged in a serious argument. This left her feeling depressed, anxious, and helpless. The topic at hand was how to keep herself from engaging with him when he had been drinking, something she felt she had to do in order to protect herself.

As we discussed this, a porcupine walked past the window she was facing. In all the years I had worked there, I had never seen a porcupine, and I have not seen one since. We talked about what the symbolic meaning could be. Sometimes I use a book of symbols and sometimes I just let the meaning come from within the person. In this case, she decided that the quills of the porcupine were a built-in protective mechanism that afforded strength and the ability to keep a distance. The porcupine can simply walk away by showing its "weapon" but without necessarily using it. She decided that the next time she had a problem with her husband, she would remember the porcupine and recognize her "weapon" was to walk away without becoming aggressive and without getting hurt. This may be an idiosyncratic interpretation, but that is exactly how synchronicity needs to be used.

Another personal example of animal synchronicity occurred many years ago. An abnormality that could have been malignant was detected in a routine medical screening test I had. It required repeating the test every six months. I was very worried when I went to the next follow-up appointment. As I drove out of my driveway, I spotted a ruby-necked pheasant crossing my path. Again, I had never seen one before and have never seen one since. But at that moment, taking in its vitality, beauty, and vibrancy, I knew I would be fine, as indeed I turned out to be. In the years of being in my "cottage" office, I have spotted rabbits, foxes, wolves, hawks, a myriad of birds and butterflies, and a most unusual snake—all seen at just the right moment to jolt me or another observer into an insight. Of course these can be seen as coincidences, but what is important is how they serve as gateways into a meaningful realization about the inner self or one's circumstances.

Body Information

The body often acts as an indicator of intuitive information. We have already discussed the importance of relaxation, but there are ways the body communicates the presence of intuition. Have you ever encountered or heard something that affected you deeply, but you first experienced the information as goose bumps? This is a response by the sympathetic nervous system, but it is triggered by strong emotions. We may not understand consciously why we respond this way, yet there is a certain "knowing" that this is something to pay attention to. Often my patients or I will experience this when they say something that rings true, which may even surprise them. When I validate their insight by calling it "truth bumps," they are able to appreciate their own wisdom and themselves as their greatest source of information. Other body indicators may be warmth, chills, aches and pains, and flutters.

Meditation

Meditation has become an important tool for clearing the busyness of our thoughts. There are many ways to meditate and many disciplines with certain criteria or rules for the proper way to meditate. In its simplest form, all that is needed is a letting go of all extraneous distractions and paying attention only to the deepest layers of the mind—in other words, being mindful. I think of mindfulness as an acute awareness of the present moment. By eliminating distracting thoughts about the past or future, we can become more receptive to that subtle voice of intuition.

Inspired by Thich Nah Hahn's book *The Miracle of Mindfulness*,[12] I have my students do a simple exercise in mindfulness. You can try it now. Put a raisin, a single raisin, in your mouth and close your eyes. Don't chew it. Let it linger in your mouth. Notice how the taste and texture change. Take your time, be mindful, and pay attention only to the raisin. When you are ready, take your time to bite into it, chew it, and then slowly swallow it.

This is a mindfulness experience in that it makes you pay attention to the details of a simple action that we usually rush right through. Try doing the same thing during a meal. You will probably notice flavors and textures that you overlooked before. This exercise will teach you how to be mindful, which you can then apply to other areas of your life. Mindfulness is akin to silence. It clears out distractions, so if there is information to be aware of, you are more likely to pay attention.

A good example that demonstrates how silence, relaxation, meditation, and body feeling work to create an opening for profound intuitive information is the story of Friedrich August Kekulé (1829–1896). Kekulé, a German organic chemist, is best known for his theory of chemical structure—in particular, how carbon atoms link to each other to form aromatic compounds. Although he did not discover it, he identified the structure of benzene. Benzene is now known to be a natural component of crude oil and is one of the most basic petrochemicals. In our industrialized world, it is used to make other chemicals that are then used to make polymers and plastics, resins and adhesives, nylon, some types of rubbers, lubricants, dyes, detergent, drugs, explosives, and pesticides.

Kekulé's identification of benzene's structure occurred in an intuitive moment. While sitting quietly by a fire, in reverie or perhaps a meditative state, he saw the flames of the fire as individual elements that formed a snake biting its own tail. This image of the snake biting its own tail is a classic ancient symbol called the *ouroboros*, whose meaning is related to its circular nature. For Kekulé, the snake became carbon atoms connected by lines. He realized that the structure of benzene could not be a straight line of carbon atoms, as it was previously thought, but was instead a circular structure, solving the mystery of aromatic compounds that had eluded chemists for years.

Looking at this story from the perspective of what we have learned so far, Kekulé, in silence, with the body relaxed, went into an Alpha wave brain pattern. This allowed for *ma*, or the space/gap, where the right brain received the intuitive information and communicated via the corpus callosum to the left brain, which knew what to do with the information, and the puzzle of organic chemistry was solved.

Art

Creativity involves, perhaps requires, intuition. Anyone who has done art of any kind—whether it is visual, writing, dance, or music—knows something about how time is experienced. When I was young, I wrote and performed my own songs. The process of writing would always transport me to an almost transcendent state where I was totally unaware of time. When I have painted, written, danced, or engaged in any other artistic endeavor, the experience has been the same.

You may also have found yourself engaged in an activity, and all of a sudden, you realize several hours have passed without your being aware. The Greeks had a word for this—*kairos*. There are actually two words for time in Greek. One is *chronos*, which refers to chronological, linear, sequential, clock-watching time—the one we experience daily and is the most familiar to us. The other is *kairos*, which is experiential time. It refers to a nonawareness of time, an indeterminate time. The word came from the name of the Greek god of opportunity and implies creating an opening and going through it. *Chronos* time is measurable while *kairos* time is not. The opening that is created—the door or the *ma*—when there is no awareness of time passing is where intuition can guide us in action and expression.

Chronos Time   Kairos Time

Mental Imagery

Most of us have the capacity to see images or symbolic representations in our mind. Even people who say they are not visual will "see" or sense images when relaxed and open. Daydreams, flights of fancy, and fantasy are all visual symbolic representations. Often these mental symbols are how intuitive information comes in. Imagining different times or cultures may be a way that we allow ourselves to become aware of information about ourselves. Sometimes stories, movies, or books may touch us in very profound ways. These may actually be clues about information in the mind-field that we cannot readily let ourselves be aware of. Intuition is subtly letting itself be known until we are ready to let the details of that information in. This type of imagery will become more meaningful when we talk about the mind-field in Part III.

The Vesica Pisces of Intuition

It should be clear by now that intuition comes in through silence, spaces, in between breaths in what may be an almost transcendent part of us. Whether we talk about dreams, synchronicity, body information, art, or mental imagery, all have something in common that appear to create a place for intuition to make itself known. What they have in common is an overlap between our physical nature and our transcendent nature. The image I use to envision this space is the *vesica pisces*, which means the bladder of a fish, or *mandorla*, which means almond shaped, and is an image of two circles that overlap to create a pointed oval in their centers.

Vesica Pisces

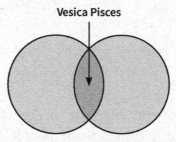

Many esoteric meanings have been assigned to this image, but here I simply look at the two overlapping circles. As human beings, we have a human nature and a divine nature, represented by the two circles. Our human nature is our physical self, our base senses, our body, our brain. Our divine nature is our spiritual self, the part that can know silence, meditation, mindfulness, and perhaps the connection to a greater intelligence or universal consciousness. The vesica pisces is the visual representation of the overlap of the two circles, of these two aspects. Perhaps it is here in the overlap that intuition comes in.

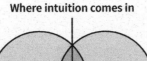

We have spent some time setting the stage by learning how to open yourself for intuitive information to come in and to be accessed. In the next chapter, we will learn what to do with intuition so that you can strengthen your abilities and learn to effectively use the intuitive information you are getting.

CHAPTER 6

WHAT TO DO WITH INTUITIVE INFORMATION

Phases of Intuition

Having intuitive information does not give us carte blanche to just say whatever we want whenever we want. I have met many people who are highly intuitive and who often feel compelled to reveal what they "see," burdened somehow by what they sense or know. Each of us needs to learn how to deal with the information and to treat it as no different from any other sensory input. We need to know how to filter, modulate, and discern information and what to do with it.

Such filtering is not always easy, especially when someone has precognizant dreams or receives information about disasters or death. This type of input may be terrifying to receive and shoulder. Knowing how to manage this ability requires intensive inner work. People who have this ability need to learn how to become objective and neutral and how to effectively use the information they receive. They will often be very depressed and may even turn to drugs as a way to block or cope with the information coming in.

This type of intuition, with such specific insight into future disasters and events, is rare and may be considered a "specialty" of sorts. Although I am not strongly precognizant in this specific way, I vividly recall a morning in 1992 when, before awakening,

I "saw" the city of Los Angeles on fire. When I woke up, it was to news of the LA riots, where indeed parts of the city had been set ablaze. If you have had these sorts of premonitions or you start to have them as you become a clearer receiver of intuitive information, it is important to not be frightened. Intuition is like tuning in to a radio frequency. You are simply receiving information. You are not responsible for it. Sometimes you may be able to give warning but often you will not. You may not know why you are the one getting the information. It may really be as random as when you scan for stations on the radio. It may help to simply realize we are all connected, making the information accessible to anyone who is sensitive enough to receive it.

To simplify how to respond to intuitive information, it helps to think of two phases of intuition.[13] The first is the *receptive* phase and involves how information is received—the intuitive "hit" or download. Reception can occur through any of our senses—hearing, sight, taste, smell, and touch—but also through psi abilities. These psi abilities include clairvoyance, clairaudience, clairsentience, telepathy, extrasensory perceptions, and psychometry. Intuition is that inner knowing. Intuitive information can also be received through emotions: anger, sadness, fear, or happiness. The second is the *dynamic* phase, or the action phase. What do we do with the intuitive information? How do we know when to say something and when to keep it to ourselves? How do we share the information?

Receptive phase	Dynamic phase
Five physical senses	Action to take
Five psi senses	Share or keep silent
Emotions	Follow three-times rule
Inner knowing	

I have learned that the number one rule to follow when considering sharing intuitive information is that, in general, it is best not to offer unsolicited information, especially if the information is vague and uncertain. It is useless to tell a person something that is abstract or something the person does not want to know. During my residency, I elected to do psychiatric work in a hospice. I had the romanticized idea that people who were dying would want to talk about their deepest spiritual feelings. I was wrong. Many people do not want to talk about these things, and I learned to respect that. I had to get better at hearing my intuition guiding me in whether or not to share information and even how to listen to better understand what a person might need. In the healing professions, it is good to offer compassion but on the patient's terms, not one's own.

As an intuitive therapist, I find it is not unusual for me to know more than what my patient has consciously brought to his or her own awareness. I once worked with someone whose most important issue I knew and could see right away. I never brought it up. It took a year of careful and respectful therapy for her to be able to see it and know it for herself and, finally, to work on it.

There are times when it may be important to share what you know. Christine Page, MD, has suggested that intuitives apply the "three-times rule:" When the information comes in, send it away. If it comes in again, send it away again. If it persists for the third time, then honor its persistence and follow or offer the information. Once, during a therapy session, I kept seeing a young boy on a bicycle. I kept ignoring the image and tried to send it away. The image and words "ask about the bicycle" persisted until finally, I found a way to do so. This turned out to be a pivotal memory in the person's life, one of which he was ashamed yet had affected him greatly. It was a memory that became significant in our work together.

Just as it is unwise to give advice unless asked, intuitive information should not be given without permission. Information cannot be imparted in an ego-centered way. It is important to be clear on who is served by the information—the giver of it or the receiver. We must ask ourselves: What is my intent in revealing this intuitive information? Above all, any information must be imparted with compassion and respect. Remember: intuition is nonjudgmental, compassionate, and detached from the outcome; therefore, we must have the wisdom to impart information in a meaningful way that will not make the recipient vulnerable. Tina Zion, a superb medical intuitive, discusses this masterfully in her book *Become a Medical Intuitive*. As a medical intuitive, Tina receives sensitive information about a person's health and body. She must not only tune in to her intuition, but also must impart it honestly and compassionately.

Intuition in Making Decisions

Up until now, I have talked about intuitive information as it relates to others, but there are times we get intuitive information about a situation or people important to ourselves. Sometimes this involves making decisions. We can use the same rules—send the intuitive message away; if it comes back, send it away again, and after the third time, pay close attention to the message. It still may be difficult to find an answer. Keep in mind if you are too close to the situation or too invested in an outcome, you may not have the clarity or objectivity to hear the intuitive guidance. In that case wait for a time when you can be still and quiet, allowing the information to come as we discussed earlier.

There are times when a decision has to be made quickly, and you cannot afford to wait for the three-times rule. For example, you might be driving, and suddenly you have a strong feeling that you should avoid your usual route. Acting on that feeling, you may later realize you avoided an accident ahead. When I was an intern in my medical training, long before I understood the mechanics of intuition or even before I had integrated my strong intuitive sense, I had an experience where intuition simply took over.

I was working on the neurology ward, my first rotation, at the very beginning of my internship. One of my first patients was a man who had suffered a severe stroke and was essentially paralyzed and unable to speak. Every day I would check on him, but I would also spend time chatting with him, letting him know everything that I was doing before I did it and why we needed the tests. I would always greet him and often just sit with him. On this particular morning, I walked into the room and immediately knew that he was having a heart attack. What was I to do? How could I go to my resident, my superior, and, without any evidence, tell her that I was sure that this patient was having a heart attack? But my hesitation did not last long. Almost without thinking, I told my resident what was happening.

Remarkably, my resident didn't hesitate either, and she supported me in calling a code, meaning getting a resuscitation team into his room. When they came and did the initial assessment, we confirmed my patient was having a heart attack. Immediate intervention was given to the patient, and soon he was transferred to the cardiac ICU. After that, the internal medicine team referred to me as the "psych intern that called the code."

I visited my patient a few times but then lost track of him, and I don't know what the final outcome was. I do know that, at least for the moment, he had been spared the more severe consequences of a heart attack. I would like to think that at least he might have had an opportunity to recover some functioning from the initial stroke. This experience became a significant validating piece in the integration of intuition into my daily functioning. I could not ignore the strength of the feeling that had been so overwhelming I had to act on it without question. It allowed me to trust that "knowing" more and more.

You will come to realize that when your own feeling is that strong, you will become more trusting of it and you will know to act on it without having to think too much about the guidelines I have set out.

Obstacles to Intuition

What keeps us from relying on intuition, since it seems to be readily available? There are many reasons we create obstacles to intuition. These include fear, denial, invalidation, self-deception, control, and willpower. Most of us have a fear of failure, of being wrong, or of humiliation. Until we really trust ourselves, we may find intuition too subtle or too ethereal to rely on. We may already be feeling insecure, and this makes us avoid the risk of trusting intuition. Equally powerful is our fear of success, which may engender expectations from others and a sense of responsibility in us.

When I was younger, my friends would call me to ask for "Helen predictions." Girlfriends wanted to know if a boy would ask them out, and boys would ask if they should date a certain girl. Despite the innocuous questions, I began to feel some sense of responsibility for what I told others. I was not as trustful of my information as I am now. If intuitive information is important, such as on matters of disease or danger, the sense of responsibility can be even greater. This may even lead us to deny the information received, or we may rationalize it in order not to trust it. We might struggle with invalidation, especially if an experience of an intuitive feeling turned out not to be accurate information. After all, just as we cannot always be sure of what we hear with our ears, see with our eyes, feel with our fingers, or taste with our mouth, so we cannot always know that our intuition is always 100 percent correct.

Sometimes we may be afraid of being discounted, especially if we are concerned with what others might think. It may feel too dangerous to break away from our "tribe." It may be difficult to trust ourselves instead of others. We may even have developed a complex series of self-deceptions to protect ourselves: these self-deceptions may take the form of habits that keep us distracted or in conflict with ourselves, the lies we tell ourselves, and the defenses we create. It may seem easier to engage in these self-deceiving behaviors than to risk judgment, rejection, or not being liked or accepted by the people around us.

Another important obstacle to intuition is the struggle we have with our willpower and our need to control. This conflict may be about what we want, what we think we want, or what we think we don't want. Most of us want to feel that we can control everything—or at least we want to control as much as possible. We want to feel safe and assured and often we will try to control as much as possible to ensure that safety. We may forget our neutrality and objectivity and convince ourselves that the information we are getting is accurate intuition. For example, there have been times when someone I was working with wanted to marry a person they were dating. Everything pointed to not doing it, but it was something they wanted to control. Often, the marriage turned out to be a disaster. Only in retrospect did the person admit they "knew" they shouldn't have married. I have come to call these warning feelings, this knowing, the "red flags" and I encourage people to be aware of them, recognize that they are an intuitive warning, and to override their desire to control the situation. Only in this way can they trust the true intuitive information trying to guide them.

We have already established the need for silence, relaxation, and surrendering the body and the brain in order to allow intuitive information in, yet there is a psychological letting go that has to occur as well. Sometimes we have to relinquish our "plan," our self-deceptions, our fears, and our need to control in order to be aware of the wiser guidance of our deepest selves.

I have already described how I met Valerie Hunt at the NICABM conference. When I had initially received the brochure for the conference, it lit up. I knew I had to go, and I was sure it was for the enhancement of my use of kinesiology in accessing unconscious information. I planned on learning more about the body, kinesiology, and the unconscious. But all of that was simply used to get me to the conference; it served as the carrot.

By following the enticement of the carrot—what I wanted—I was led to something much greater and more important for my own growth and self-awareness—the study and understanding of intuition, bioenergy fields, the mind-field, and emotions. The carrot led me to Valerie Hunt, EdD; Christine Page, MD; Judith Orloff, MD; Mona Lisa Schulz, MD; Carolyn Myss; Norm Shealy, MD; and others—people whom I consider important in my evolution. These were my greatest teachers of intuition, bioenergy, and expanded consciousness. By relinquishing my control and surrendering to the intuition, I got to where I really needed to be. That is the beauty of the carrot and the reason it is so important for you also to be aware of your own obstacles that keep you from hearing and trusting your own intuitive voice.

Developing Intuitive Skills

I have devoted time to helping you understand intuition as thoroughly as possible because I believe that intuition leads us deeper into the mind-field and acts as the conduit for accessing the information that is there. Knowing the neurology, biology, and nature of intuition, how can one develop and enhance one's own intuitive skills? I have already given you some guidelines for developing intuitive skills, and I summarize them here:

1. Become self-aware by observing yourself through mind-fulness and meditation.

2. Pay attention to the little things, and at the same time, learn to get a read on the larger picture, the gestalt of an experience or situation, or even just a thought or feeling.

3. Take internal inventory by asking authentic self-questions and by being real with your answers. What are authentic self-questions? These are questions you ask yourself that will hone in on what you really feel, think, and want. (Some examples are included in the exercises at the end of this part.) Don't try to fool yourself by denying, resisting, or censoring the answers. They need to be asked independently of anyone or anything else around you. I don't mean to suggest that you should be self-absorbed or narcissistic; rather, be clear about yourself. How you act may end up taking into account others, but do it consciously and with awareness about yourself.

4. Practice problem-solving by breathing, relaxing, getting focused, and allowing your mind to give you information through your body, your senses, imagery, symbols, and metaphors.

5. Be aware of what is trying to come in when you begin to censor, judge, or discount information. Learn to know how to trust your yes/no answers, whether through kinesiology or by imagining check boxes and seeing which one gets checked as an answer. You can journal your experiences, paying attention to feelings and emotions.

Try all of these things. Test yourself. You will make mistakes. Be forgiving of yourself and the process. Even so, learn to trust the information and treat it as valid. Remember, all information is valid. At first you may want to reject or question it. With practice you will be increasingly reinforced, validated, and comfortable with trusting your intuition until it becomes a seamless part of your information-gathering system, just as your visual, auditory, and other sensory input is. Learning to trust and use intuition can enrich your life and take you to a much higher level of self-awareness.

Everyone is intuitive. Intuition is a powerful source of information, worth learning to trust. Intuition can elevate and expand your consciousness and your self-awareness so that you can live in your fullest capacity as a divine, full-spectrum human being. You are in this life for a reason. Use your intuition to transcend your fears and live your life with complete intention and meaning.

Exercises for Developing Your Intuition

Developing Intuitive Skills

I recommend that for these insight questions and visualizations you keep a journal. Your thoughts and insights do not have to be recorded in a formal journal book or in a particular format. Rather, the goal is to track where you are when you start. Later, when you revisit these insight questions and visualizations, you can see where the experience takes you. Another reason to record your experiences is that your immediate thoughts or images may not make sense until a later time.

Insight Questions

Authentic self-awareness questions:

How do I really feel right now? What is the source of this feeling or emotion?

If I really trusted myself at this moment, what would I do? What would I say?

If I imagine looking back at the end of my life, what would I regret not having done?

Things You Can Practice Doing

1. Learn problem-solving by getting centered, focused, and receptive to breathing and relaxation. Then allow your mind to give you imagery, symbols, metaphors, body sensations, or any other sensory modality.

2. Be open to synchronicity working in your life.

3. Daydream, doodle, brainstorm, and jot down words or phrases that come to you when you have questions.

4. Play games. Don't take the process too seriously. Guess what someone you are meeting will be wearing or what a new place you are going to will look like. Doing this may seem simple and mundane, but it is like flexing muscles to strengthen them. As you begin to see how accurate you are, you will gain confidence when other types of intuitive information come in.

5. Get physical! Yoga, tai chi, walking, swimming—all help to keep a clear and open mind, and that allows for clearer intuitive information to come in. If you can't do these things, at least stretch your body, even if you are at a desk.

6. Stretch your creative muscles; you don't have to make great works of art, so be free in your expressions. Don't be afraid to doodle or play with crayons or clay (even Play-Doh). Write whatever you feel like writing. (I am especially fond

of Julia Cameron's "morning pages," which she describes in *The Artist's Way*. She suggests writing three pages in the morning before you do anything else, without thought to what you are writing. This is what we, in my field, call stream of consciousness and can be creatively liberating.)

7. Spend time in nature.

8. Cultivate and learn to enjoy silence and solitude. You don't have to go to a monastery. This may be as simple as turning everything off—the TV, radio, all the streaming devices— and tuning in internally, staying aware to the experience.

9. Become more mindful. You can do this in simple ways. Every now and then when you eat, do it slowly, paying attention to how the food smells, tastes, and feels in your mouth as you chew. When you wash dishes, pay attention to the sound and the feel of the water. There are so many routine activities that you can practice mindfulness with.

10. Accept mistakes related to your intuition with humor and grace. Sometimes we just get it wrong, and sometimes we are not meant to know. Often we get it right, but we ignore it and later realize it was a mistake to have done so. What is important to remember is everything is an opportunity to learn about yourself, to go deeper, to become more aware.

11. Learn to trust the information that does come, and treat it as valid.

12. Be grateful for all the information that comes to you. It is part of your growth and will allow you to see yourself and everything around you with an open mind and heart.

How to Strengthen Intuition by Keeping a Journal

1. Keep the entries simple; sometimes they may be no more than bullets.

2. Keep track of impressions, thoughts, or feelings that come spontaneously.

3. Pay attention to and document synchronistic events.

4. Be especially aware of and write about blocks you experience—fear, denial, self-deception, willpower, your need for control—and how they play out.

5. Write about what you experience in quiet moments.

6. Record your dreams as soon as you wake up.

Guided Visualizations and Meditations

These are meditations or guided imagery for developing your intuition. You may want to read the visualization out loud while recording it so that you can follow it comfortably later.

Meet Your Intuition

You will begin by opening and preparing your energy field, which helps to open your mind-field where intuitive information comes in:

1. Close your eyes, take a deep breath.

2. Breathe through the bottom of your feet, in through your left and out through the right.

3. Breathe through your knees, through your elbows, through your shoulders.

4. Next, breathe into the major energy centers using specific

colors. Begin at the space between your legs, and breathe the color red.

5. Breathe in through the area around your pubic bone in the color orange.

6. Breathe your belly in the color yellow.

7. Breathe through your heart in the color green. Feel the warmth and openness there.

8. Breathe through your throat in the color blue.

9. Go to the top of your head, and breathe in a crystal-clear white.

10. Connect fully with your body. Release every tension in your body.

Start by imagining yourself on a walk. See the path you are on. Notice what it looks like. Notice details. Is there water? Are there animals? Trees or sand? Take your time to notice the details.

Soon you will come to a clearing where you will find a structure, your structure, your house, which we will call your house of consciousness. It does not have to look like a traditional house. It can be whatever you want it to be, real or fantasy or from your imagination. It may remind you of a place you have been to before or have seen in pictures. It may defy gravity or lack architectural sense.

Notice details: windows, doors, the exterior. What is it made of? What color is it? Are there plants outside? Can you feel a breeze or smell the ocean? Notice what it is like for you. It is your very own place, not anyone else's, a beautiful place of safety and comfort, of nurturing that feels inviting and welcoming. It is your house of consciousness.

Go inside your house. As you enter, notice the interior. Notice details, paying attention to things you like, such as appealing colors, decorations that please you, and whether or not there are furnishings. It may be antique in style or modern. It can be anything you want, real or from your imagination. Whatever you want it to be, make it be so that you feel very comfortable and at peace.

Now invite your intuition to join you. It may take any form, but notice the presence, what it feels like, what you feel. Welcome and greet your intuition. Your communication may not be in words. It may be telepathic or in symbols, imagery, or any other sensory modality. Take time with this part of yourself, your highest, wisest, most profound self. In this deep, silent space, ask your intuition, "What do I most need to know or be aware of right now?" You might have a problem that you are trying to solve or a situation for which you need guidance. Or you may choose to wait and receive whatever information your intuition offers you.

After this communication with your intuition, rest quietly and open yourself to other information that might come. Notice any thought, feeling, or image that comes to you in response. Just notice whatever comes in and be with it for a little while. It's not necessary to understand or interpret it. Just be receptive. You will get information. There is no need to filter, censor, or judge it. Simply be open and accept what comes in.

You may feel like you are making something up. That's okay. Even if you have chosen to make it up, what you experience has meaning and significance for you if you simply accept and pay attention to it. Allow whatever is happening to happen.

You may feel that nothing is happening, or that you are getting nothing. That's okay too. Don't *try* to make something happen—trying gets in the way of the process. If nothing is coming to you, make sure you are not anxious, tense, or filtering. If you still don't get anything, it is not a failure. It may not be the right time. Accept that and realize something may come to you after this exercise—maybe even when you are in your car, or tonight before you go to sleep, or in the next few days. Trust that what you are experiencing is exactly the right thing for you in this place and at this time. Whatever thoughts, feelings, and images you do get, allow yourself to sit with them for a while.

Before you leave, your intuition will give you a gift, a token, something to take back with you to reassure you and remind you of what you have experienced. Receive that gift now. When you feel complete with the process, prepare to leave your house. Thank your intuition and know that you can come back whenever you wish. It is always available to you.

Leave your house of consciousness and walk on the path, making your way back to where you started. As you begin the journey back, know that you can return at any time. It is yours. It is a place to find comfort, peace, and answers, where you can know and be with the deepest part of yourself.

Begin to notice your breath again. Pay attention to how your body is feeling, and become aware of your surroundings. When you are ready, come back to the room and open your eyes. Now take time to briefly write down your experience.

Intuition Self-Assessment

After an exercise, a dream, a reverie, or any experience that you feel is trying to guide you, I suggest you do the following:

Ask yourself these questions, then describe and write your answers as if you were talking to a friend.

- What questions were answered?

- What questions do I still have?

- What did I experience physically?

- What did I experience emotionally?

- What was the hardest part of the exercise?

- What new perspectives and insights have I gained?

- What is the potential for my growth from this experience?

TRUE VOICE[14]

Tell your story.

First to yourself.

Start with a whisper, but listen with your heart and hear the truth of all that you are.

Trust your story.

Find its meaning, understanding that a story has no beginning and no end, only a continuation of what is.

Listen carefully, desire to hear well, desire to know.

For in this way you will find what matters most.

You may believe that you are not enough, but know that you are exactly what is needed for yourself for where you are at this moment in time.

The wounds—the losses and disappointments that you have suffered—are part of your fabric, not an excuse to keep you from your greatness.

Do not be distracted by the stories others have told you about yourself, the ones that have made you believe you are small.

To make yourself small is to hear the voice of fear.

Fear of all the potential within you.

Fear, not that you may fail, but that you may succeed, that you may be more powerful and divine than you can imagine.

Challenge yourself to hear the truth, to feel deeply and passionately.

Challenge yourself to live your life fully.

A life where your voice is heard.

A life where you allow your light to shine so that others may see in their darkness.

Tell your true story, believe it, and the story that you tell will become part of the fabric of the world, restoring wholeness, compassion, healing, and love.

PART II

THE
HUMAN BIOENERGY FIELD

Everything that is, is energy.
—Albert Einstein

CHAPTER 7

INTRODUCTION TO THE HUMAN BIOENERGY FIELD

Part I focused on intuition as a way to hear the information in the mind and the mind-field. Before we learn about the mind-field, we need to lay the groundwork by examining what the human bioenergy field is. In Part II, we will look at how the human bioenergy field has been defined traditionally, the physiology and neurology that explain it, the physics and mechanics of it, and why it is important.

Bios means life; *energy* means force or work. *Human bioenergy* means human life-force. A *field* is defined as a space in which a given effect exists. Thus, the human bioenergy field is a space where there is a life-force present. This space was identified even in ancient times. Our ancestors recognized energy emanating from the body. They gave it meaning and importance, both physical and mystical. With chemistry, physics, and biology, these ancient ideas—which were based on observation, subjective feeling, and speculation—can be refined to an increasingly tangible, verifiable, and quantitative degree.

As our methods for studying and measuring this energy field improve, we understand more about this field, why it exists, and who we are as energetic beings. The human bioenergy field serves a meaningful purpose, affecting who we are, how healthy we are, and how we live our lives. We will start with and build on the basics to develop skills for identifying and working with this field.

Cultural and Traditional Ideas

Since recorded history, there have been people who could see and describe light emissions from the body. Most cultures had and still have a name for these light emissions. The Chinese use *qi* or *chi*; the Japanese, *ki*; and we say "aura." In Greek it is called *bios*; in the Hindu culture, *prana* or *shakti*; the Tibetans say *lung*; in old English it was known as *aethe*, and in Hebrew, *kuch ha guf*; in the Mayan language, it is known as *l'ol*, which means vibration or consciousness; and the Sufi use *lataif-e-sitta*. These cultures, as well as the Ethiopian, Native American, and Egyptian, recognize some form of energy emanating from the body, and most have a multicenter system of energy. All describe the human bioenergy field.

The best-known system of body energy involves seven energy centers or seven *niduses* (sites where something is formed or originated) of energy, commonly called the *chakras*. It is believed that the earliest descriptions of chakras are found in the Vedas, the most ancient religious text of India written as early as 2000–600 BC.[15] Chakra means "wheel" in Sanskrit, but it is often associated with a metaphor for the sun or the circle of life. Traditionally, and with some physiologic foundation that will be covered later, the chakras are described as circular or spiral, and are associated with certain colors and meanings.

Each chakra is usually defined by a particular color and has been given a particular meaning. The first chakra is the *root*, associated with the color red, and located at the base of the spine. It is related to the physical, to survival, the urge to live, and grounding. The second chakra is the *sacral*, associated with the color orange, and located at the lower abdomen and the pubis. It is related to power, sexuality, relationships, culture, rules, and family. The third is the *solar plexus*, associated with the color yellow, and located just above the navel. It is related to emotions, sense of self, self-esteem, discipline, and personal empowerment.

The fourth chakra is the *heart*, associated with the color green and located on the center left side of the chest. This chakra is related to love, silence, meditation, and integration of the opposites. The fifth is the *throat*, which is associated with the color blue and related to creativity, imparting and receiving knowledge, listening, and communicating. The sixth is the *brow*, located in the center of the forehead, between the eyebrows, and is associated with the color violet. It is sometimes called the third eye and is related to intuition, filtering and understanding the outside world, imaging, and bringing ideas into reality or manifesting. The seventh and last major chakra is the *crown*, associated with the color white, and it has to do with highest consciousness and connection to the divine.

In general, we can see that the lower three chakras have to do with life and the physical while the upper three chakras have to do with higher ideals, such as the spiritual and divine. The middle chakra, the heart, is the bridge between the physical and the spiritual.

These seven chakras or energy centers have been referred to together as the human aura. The aura is usually associated with the sixties' new-age, hippie-dippy, metaphysical ideas. But there is a reason that the aura is visible to some, and with our increasing knowledge and comprehension, we can take it out of the realm of the "woo-woo" and into an important new model for defining, identifying, and treating dysfunction in the human body and mind. We will need a bit of a science lesson, including some chemistry, to understand what energy is; some biology and neurology to answer why seven chakras were identified in the first place; and physics to learn what the mechanics of the bioenergy field are.

Understanding science as it pertains to the human bioenergy

field allows you to grasp the methods to work with your own field. The simple exercises you will learn will allow you to maintain your field's balance and improve functioning. You will also get a glimpse of what the future holds for improving instrumentation that will allow us to verify and measure the bioenergy field, thereby opening the way for new research to validate what we can now only hypothesize.

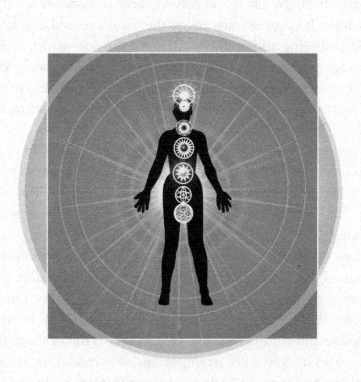

CHAPTER 8

A LITTLE SCIENCE

Much is still emerging and being uncovered when it comes to the science of the human bioenergy field. An increasing number of scientists, especially physicists and cell biologists, are working to refine what the bioenergy field is, but Valerie Hunt, EdD, was one of the early leaders in proposing hypotheses about the science of the bioenergy field. Many of the explanations for the scientific constructs of the human bioenergy field came from her research and quest. I have found that her explanations, even though simplified and not thoroughly researched, are a good starting point, and more sophisticated research and explanations are emerging. There are many in the field of neuroscience and quantum physics who immerse themselves in rigorous research on the mechanics of the human bioenergy field. Among them, Claude Swanson, PhD, a quantum physicist, has compiled a comprehensive examination and description of historical and most up-to-date research available related to the bioenergy field, energy medicine, and consciousness.[16]

Let's start with a little bit of chemistry and physics in order to understand the physical structure of the bioenergy field. Chemistry is the science of matter at the atomic and molecular level. Physics is the science of matter, its motion through space and time, and energy and force. The focus of physics can be on atoms and their electrons, interactions between the particles that make up the nucleus of atoms, and interactions within the nucleus. What is of relevance to us is that all these interactions involve energy, and energy is integral to learning about the human bioenergy field.

What Atoms Do

Atoms are the building blocks of all things. They are made of electricity, which is the source of all energy. All matter is made up of atoms, and all atoms have similarities but are not identical. What makes the difference between an inanimate object and an animate one is the instruction and the stimuli that the atoms receive. A rock radiates an electrical energy based upon a structure of atoms that is not complex or dynamic. The energy emanating from it will be relatively predictable and unchanging. We can predict how heat or pressure will affect it. An animate, living being is dynamic and changing. It radiates a more complex atomic energy from the atoms of the different organs, muscles, connective tissue, nerves, and cells within the body.

The more complex the being—like the human being—the more dynamic and changing this atomic energy will be. A human, after all, is a bunch of atoms making up cells. These cells organize into systems, and the systems organize into the body. Atoms cannot do anything without stimulus, whether that stimulus is simple, like heat or pressure, or more complex, like emotions. The nature of the stimulus determines whether the electrons within atoms spin fast, slowly, or on and off. Though the cause of the spinning of atoms may still be somewhat of a mystery, we could say it is life itself—particularly the experiences, thoughts, and emotions we have throughout life–that generate energy. For more on this idea that experiences, thoughts, emotions carry an energy which affects the cells at the most fundamental atomic level, I refer you to Bruce Lipton and his seminal work described in *The Biology of Belief*.[17]

To understand better what is happening, we need to know the structure of an atom. An atom is a collection of little pieces of electricity that come from neutrons, protons, and electrons. Its center, the nucleus, contains protons, which carry a positive electrical charge, and neutrons, which carry no electrical charge. Around the nucleus there are electrons, which have a negative electrical charge.

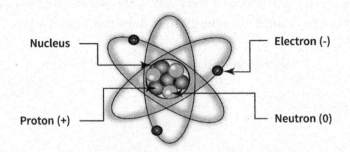

When there are equal numbers of electrons, protons, and neutrons, the atom has no charge and is neutral. But atoms are not all alike—they are dynamic, and they are not all neutral. When an atom gains or loses an electron, it becomes an ion. There are two types of ions: positive—in which the atom lost an electron and is now positively charged—and negative—in which the atom gained an electron and is now negatively charged.

Sometimes an atom has an unpaired electron, or one electron in an orbit by itself. Such an atom is then called a free radical. Free radicals should not be confused with ions. Although a free radical has at least one unpaired electron, it does not carry a charge like an ion because the number of *orbiting* electrons still matches the number of protons in the nucleus, resulting in an overall neutral charge. The presence of some free radicals is healthy for our body, but too many free radicals can lead to cell and tissue damage, contributing to many diseases.

Positive and negative ions do not behave the same way. Positive ions follow a course around every cell and tissue—they are not random. They are not as active as negative ions; they are slower and tend to stay in the body until they find an electron with which to pair. Negative ions are more active. Negative ions radiate from the inside of the body. Although there are both negative and positive ions everywhere on the body, the body surface retains the more sluggish positive ions. When the negative ions make their way to the surface of the body, they attract the positive ions, generating a "cloud" of energy that does not float away.

Negative ions radiate from the inside of the body
toward the surface.

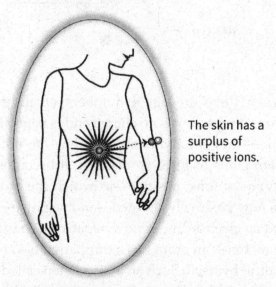

The skin has a surplus of positive ions.

This is what we think of as the "aura" or the human bioenergy field. The human bioenergy field is an electrical field.

This electrical energy is a field, what our ancestors identified as the human aura, and what we will call the human bioenergy field. This idea of the origin of the aura may not be all there is. As our understanding becomes more sophisticated through research in quantum physics, other hypotheses have been given for what generates the aura. The most intriguing and supported is related to the creation of torsion fields, also referred to as toric or torus fields.

DNA within the cells and some larger biomolecules of the body emit particles or packets of energy seen as light called biophotons. These stay predominantly inside the body where their energy is stored for biochemical functions. However, some biophotons leave the body in the form of what are called torsion waves. Torsion waves occur when there is a change in the spin of the electron. The escaping particles carry information about the cells from which they were emitted. This information is holographic, meaning an identical representation of the original. The torsion waves carry the same information as the particles, and the unique pattern created by all the torsion waves creates a torsion field carrying information. This field is equivalent to the aura or bioenergy field. So when we talk about electrons on the surface of skin, if we go deeper into quantum physics we find torsion waves, and from there we will leave it to physicists like Dr. Swanson to explain how the torsion field validates what has been known about energy healing for centuries. The main point is that what we call the aura is a *field* and as such does not have defined boundaries.

Every energy system has a positive and a negative charge generated by the atoms when they spin. As these electrical charges spin, they also produce a magnetic field. Thus, we can also think of the bioenergy field as an *electromagnetic* field. When the negative charge is equal to or more than the positive, then the electrical force is equal to or greater than the magnetic, allowing for a good flow of energy. When the positive charge is greater than the negative, excessive amounts of free radicals are generated and the magnetic force is greater than the electrical, indicating a disturbance in the body, and disrupting the flow of energy.

Becoming Grounded

Have you ever noticed that when you are at the beach, walking along barefoot on the sand, you feel healthier, more robust, and energetic? This experience is actually a signal that the ions in your field are becoming stabilized or grounded. The earth's crust, sea air, oceans, and mountains all have a surplus of negative ions. When your body surface (which, remember, has more positive ions) comes in contact with these negative ions, the result is a field that is grounded or in balance. It is being grounded that contributes to a positive sense of well-being.

You can try it yourself and see how you feel. Take fifteen minutes to walk or sit with your bare feet touching the ground—dirt, grass, sand. The excess of negative ions of the ground will bind with the excess of positive ions of your skin. From what you already have learned, you know that this will neutralize or bring into balance the charge of the atoms and ground your bioenergy field.

I once worked with a teacher who was becoming increasingly frustrated with her classes and with students who seemed uninterested and unengaged. I suggested that, if at all possible, she should take the children outside and have them sit with bare feet on the ground. Fortunately, she was in a school where she was able to do so and came back reporting that the activity had improved everyone's humor and functioning. Of course, I cannot say for certain that being barefoot on the ground or just a change of pace caused the improvement, but it is hard to argue that most of us feel recharged and renewed when we come in contact with nature.

There are still many details we do not know about the energy systems of the body. As our human mind evolves, what we are able to understand about the subtle energy that is the bioenergy field increases. We have already extended our capacity beyond our senses into the science of quantum physics. Every step closer is an evolution, not just in our learning, but in our consciousness.

The Biology of the Human Bioenergy Field

Let's continue building on our knowledge of the human bioenergy field by learning why it has traditionally been identified by the seven energy centers known as chakras. To do this, we will look at the biology of the body.

The neuromuscular system is itself an electromagnetic system triggered by biological and emotional stimuli. There are several components of the neurological system. A *neuron* is an excitable cell in the nervous system that processes and transmits information by electrochemical signaling. When numerous neurons are bundled and connected together, they form a biological mass of tissues called *ganglia*. When ganglia interconnect with each other, they form a complex system or network of intersecting nerves and ganglia called a *plexus*. Think of it like wires. Instead of just one wire, there are several wires bundled together. A plexus has a stronger and more intense electrical impulse because there are many wires, or ganglia, bundled together. The entire system is protected if there is damage in one wire by having numerous backup wires. In the body, these bundled wires or neural networks called a plexus are where they are needed most, the major organs and glands. There are seven major plexuses that work to communicate electrical impulses. These function as follows:

1. The *cervical* plexus serves the head, neck, and shoulders.

2. The *brachial* plexus serves the chest, shoulders, and arms.

3. The *celiac* plexus serves the internal organs.

4. The *myenteric* (Auerbach's) plexus is associated with the gastrointestinal tract.

5. The *lumbar* plexus serves the back, abdomen, groin, thighs, knees, and calves.

6. The *sacral* plexus serves the pelvis, buttocks, genitals, thighs, calves, and feet.

7. The *coccygeal* plexus is associated with the region over the coccyx (tailbone).

Overlaps in the areas served by different plexuses can be explained by the anatomical complexity of the system. Some plexuses specialize in innervating muscles (spinal plexus innervates the lumbosacral, or lower, region of the spine) while others specialize in innervating organs (autonomic plexus innervates the abdominal or pelvic organs). For our purposes, we just want to look at a very broad picture of where there are larger networks of nerves generating electrical impulses, which manifest as energy. If we now look at the chakras, we see their location correlates closely with the location of plexus (think large concentration of nerve fibers) and specific organs:

1. The *base* or first chakra is located at the base of the coccyx (tailbone) and correlates to the external sex organs.

2. The *sacral* or second chakra is associated with the ovaries/testes, sexuality, and procreation.

3. The *abdomen* or third chakra is associated with the pancreas, liver, spleen, stomach, and adrenals. It is related to digestion and clearing toxins.

4. The *heart* or fourth chakra is associated with the thymus gland and is related to the immune system and stress.

5. The *throat* or fifth chakra is associated with the thyroid gland and is related to the metabolism, growth, and maturation of the human body.

6. The *brow* or sixth chakra is associated with the pineal gland,

which is related to the sleep-wake cycle and the production of melatonin.

7. The *crown* or seventh chakra is associated with the pituitary gland and is important in the production and regulation of hormones that determine homeostasis in the body.

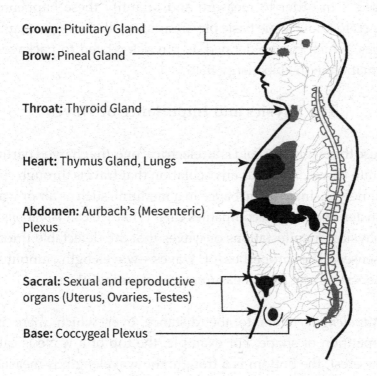

Crown: Pituitary Gland

Brow: Pineal Gland

Throat: Thyroid Gland

Heart: Thymus Gland, Lungs

Abdomen: Aurbach's (Mesenteric) Plexus

Sacral: Sexual and reproductive organs (Uterus, Ovaries, Testes)

Base: Coccygeal Plexus

The seven-energy chakra system was recognized because each of the chakras corresponds to the location of ganglia and plexus that serve the body's most important organs or glands. These areas emanate the strongest electrical energy. People with acute senses can detect these stronger signals through seeing colors or having other variations in sensations such as warmth, coolness, or tingling.

Our ancestors didn't have todays' instruments and relied only on their senses (including intuitive and psi abilities); they could sense the "hottest" areas of internal energy. Today's bodyworkers and those trained in the subtle detection of energy can feel changes and variations in these energy centers, the chakras, and people who see energy will see the strongest signals at those locations.

What happens in the bioenergy field that allows it to be "sensed"? In order to measure and quantify these happenings, we need to know some basic physics, especially biologic quantum physics, which can be defined as physics related to packages of information in the bioenergy field.

The Physics and Importance of Waves

Because the bioenergy field is an electrical one, the charged particles generate waves. A *wave* is an oscillation that travels through space and time, causing a disturbance in a medium, such as air or water. A transfer of energy accompanies this. What we call *vibrations* are the physical manifestations of waves that are detectable through the senses. The properties of waves—wavelength, amplitude, frequency—make their measurements meaningful.

Wavelength refers to the distance over which there is a repetition of shape. For example, the top of a wave is called the crest, the bottom is a trough; the wavelength is measured from crest to crest or trough to trough.

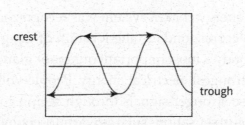

Amplitude refers to how strong or big the wave is.

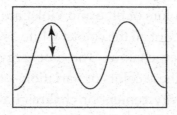

Frequency is how many waves are made in a period of time. There are low, middle, and high frequencies. The following are measured over one second of time.

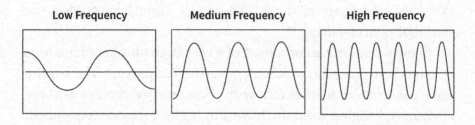

Frequencies and amplitudes occur with color and sound. Color is made of light waves. In the color spectrum, the frequency of waves increases from low to high. Red is the lowest, and violet is the highest. In between are orange, yellow, green, and blue. White is the sum of all colors and reflects all the colors of the visible light spectrum to the eyes.

Chakras radiate energy waves with various frequencies. Since color is also defined by frequencies, we can extrapolate that the frequency waves of chakras or specific energy centers have specific colors. In Chapter 9 I describe research that has been done in recording the frequency patterns of the chakras.

The reason color is associated with chakra energy centers is related to the vibration frequency, which generates wave patterns seen in that spectrum of color. The lowest frequency colors, red and orange, are in the lower energy centers; the middle frequency colors of yellow and green are in the central energy centers; the highest frequency colors of blue and violet are in the higher ones; the highest frequency of all the colors, white, is at the crown. These account for the seven chakras. The bioenergy field or aura as a whole may radiate these colors or variations of color.

Because the energy centers or chakras have this property of waves with frequency variations, there are other ways to detect them. Sound also creates waves. Christof Koch, PhD, is a professor of biology and engineering at the California Institute of Technology where he heads the KLAB (Koch lab). He is a biophysicist who has devoted himself to elucidating the neural basis of consciousness. With his colleagues at the KLAB in Cal Tech, he recorded the sound of neurons firing.[18]

Energy centers are composed of a very high number of neurons (grouped into ganglia, which are grouped into plexus). There is the same association acoustically with these energy centers as there is visually, ranging from the lowest to highest sound frequencies. These are important data because now we have a basis for not just sensing the colors but also for hearing the sound that the energy centers make, allowing us to record, measure, document, and even set them to music. Valerie Hunt did just that in her *Music of Light* recordings.[19] In the next chapter, I will describe some of her visionary work and the contribution she made towards understanding the human bioenergy field.

CHAPTER 9

SOUND AS MEDICINE

Valerie Hunt and Instrumentation

After reading the scientific background information, you may see the possibility for the development of new ideas about the human bioenergy field; you may even see the possibility of creating the instruments that support those ideas. We need to take what has been traditionally discounted as fringe, esoteric, or metaphysical ideas into verifiable, reproducible, and applicable data. Even though we are all intuitive, some have more acute areas of sensitivity and perception; not everyone can read, see, or feel an aura or chakra energy. If we can develop an instrument to duplicate, measure, and record this information, we may achieve a tool that is accessible to all for identifying frequency patterns that occur in the body. This could lead to instruments that would identify the factors that affect our health and well-being by using the bioenergy field as an indicator.

Knowledge about the heart evolved in a similar manner. First, someone sensed a pulsing in the body of all living organisms. Then someone studied it—put his ear to the chest and heard rhythmic thumping. Ideas about the science of the heart evolved from Aristotle, to Galen, to da Vinci, to Harvey. With an understanding of the anatomy, physiology, and physics of the heart, there came the development of instrumentation: the electrocardiograph (EKG) with the capacity to measure and record the pulsing and the rhythms of the heart. Increasingly more detailed data were amassed to enhance echocardiography, sonograms, MRIs, and evolving instrumentation. This has been done with many organ systems, including the muscles and the brain.

What has kept us from developing these instruments to record, measure, and quantitate the bioenergy field? To answer this question, let us examine how the body and the bioenergy field differ electrically. We have numerous instruments that detect and measure electrical impulses that occur in millivolts, or one-thousandth of a volt. In terms of frequency, a millivolt has 0 to 450 cycles per second. The EKG measures the heart's electrical impulses. It gives us information on the rate and regularity of heartbeats, the size and position of the chambers of the heart, and the presence of any damage to the heart. The electroencephalograph (EEG) records the brain's spontaneous electrical activity, giving us information about the function of the brain and whether or not there is a seizure disorder or encephalopathy. The electromyograph (EMG) evaluates and records the electrical potential produced by muscle cells when those cells are electrically or neurologically activated to give us information about the health or diseases of skeletal muscles. These are all measurable because the instruments have been designed to detect millivolts.

The bioenergy field also has detectable electrical activity, but the electrical impulses occur in microvolts. That is one-millionth of a volt. In terms of frequency, a microvolt has 500 to 2,400 cycles per second. This frequency has always been detectable but was called "white noise" and was considered a dispensable, garbled sound. There appeared to be no need to try to discern the variations in white noise or make any sense of it, and later medical instruments were designed specifically to filter out this white noise.

Early in her career, Valerie Hunt became curious about that white noise and how it related to the healing process, altered states, and chakras. Working with engineers at UCLA, she created a prototype for one of the first instruments that could record the bioelectrical energy emanating from the body surface, proving that this energy occurred in frequencies thousands of times higher than any previously known electrical activity in the body.

A Scientist-Mystic

I have already referred many times to Valerie Hunt (1918–2014). Much of the revolutionary thinking about the bioenergy field over the years is still attributable to her research and writings. Dr. Hunt consulted for NASA, served with the US Department of Health, Education, and Welfare, taught courses in twenty medical colleges and universities, and held professorates at the University of Iowa, Columbia University, and UCLA. From 1948 to 1981, she was a professor at UCLA's Department of Physiologic Sciences, and later she was awarded the status of professor emerita at UCLA. She earned international acclaim in the fields of physiology, medicine, and bioengineering, and was named in the Marquis Who's Who lists for America (American Women) and the World (Education, Medicine, and Healthcare and Science and Engineering).

Traveling extensively throughout the world, she studied cultures, spirituality, and bioenergy. She researched ritualistic healing and mystical beliefs, especially in Asia, South America, Africa, and the Pacific Islands, amassing a tremendous wealth of knowledge about humanity and the human psyche. She was perceived to be not only a rigorous scientist but a mystic as well. She achieved profound experiences of spirituality and the soul, thus reaching an extraordinary level of expanded consciousness. She was a passionate educator, researcher, and author, writing numerous works to describe her process and theories.

In the 1970s while at UCLA, she became interested in the white noise picked up by medical instruments, which she identified as the aura, or the human bioenergy field. She became especially interested in the fluctuations that occurred in various emotional conditions. These were the earliest research and protocols for the relationship between energy field disturbances, disease, emotional pathologies, human field communication, and the energy spectrum of consciousness. Her findings drove her to dedicate herself to the creation of an instrument analogous to the EKG that would detect, record, document, and measure the electrical activity of the body's high-frequency bioenergy field—an instrument that could measure and record the frequencies of the human bioenergy field emanating from the surface of the human body in microvolts.[20]

Dr. Hunt's early attempts were relatively successful, and she committed herself to refining this instrument in order for it to become a viable, accessible diagnostic tool. The measurements from this instrument could potentially identify dynamic transactions between our environment and ourselves and how these transactions affect our behavior, emotions, health, illness, and disease. Her research had the potential to take us beyond our current understanding of emotions and the psyche that is based on chemical, neurological, or physiological behavior alone.

Although she came close to creating this instrument, the prototype being the Hunt Bioenergy Field Meter, the limitations of technology kept her from completing it before the end of her life. She laid the foundation; research continues on the development and efficacy of similar instruments. Gaetan Chevalier, PhD, an atomic physicist and engineer who worked with Dr. Hunt, continues the research of these types of instruments as the director of the Earthing Institute and research director of Psy-Tek Subtle Energy Laboratory.[21] There are engineers, scientists, and visionaries throughout the world working to develop similar instruments to accurately detect the variant frequencies of the human bioenergy field so that in the future we may have additions to our arsenal of diagnostic and treatment tools.

Music of Light

Using the equipment available at the time, including transistors, oscillators, and microphones, and working with a former NASA engineer, Dr. Hunt was able to make a bioenergy-field instrument that isolated the strongest radiating bioenergy groups by their frequency patterns. In essence, she recorded the sound of the chakras or energy centers. She realized that the bioenergy field of the listener would *entrain*, or synchronize, to the frequency of what is heard. In other words, specific areas of the field—the lower, midrange, and higher—have an effect on the body that could be induced by listening to corresponding sound frequencies. For example, the red, orange, and yellow frequencies of the lower centers with their lower frequency are vitalizing, while the blue, mauve, and violet high frequencies of the higher centers induce relaxation.

The *Music of Light* CDs, which are the result of this research, are a wonderful tool for energizing or calming the body. The sounds themselves seem like distortions in the air, high- and low-pitched buzzing and humming sounds. Dr. Hunt set these sounds to music. By listening to the catalogue of music available, with the music in one ear and the bioenergy-field sounds in the other, she painstakingly correlated classical, contemporary, and other music genres with the sound of energy-center vibrations. The result was a blending of one with the other. As a result, listening to the African drumbeats of the lower frequency can have the same effect as a good strong cup of coffee, while "Moonlight Sonata" can put you into a very relaxed, restful state. A compilation of the entire spectrum together can make the entire body feel refreshed and grounded. Keep in mind that the calming or energizing effects are not caused by the music alone but by the particular frequencies of sound waves from the energy centers, which are instructing, or entraining, the cells.

Entrainment means that there is synchronization to an external stimulus. This entrainment leads to a coherency of energy flow where the energy is flowing smoothly without obstruction, something we will discuss in more depth in Chapter 10. For example, if every muscle in your body is tense, your frequencies are completely chaotic. When you listen to "Moonlight Sonata" combined with the higher frequencies, you start to feel calm. You can liken it to this scenario: you are in an anxious state, and you visit a friend whose environment is peaceful and who always has a cup of tea at the ready. What happens? The more powerful, calming, reassuring energy of your friend is instructing your chaotic energy, telling your cells to synchronize with the more powerful, calming frequencies, and you end up feeling calmer yourself. Medical models explain this synchronization in terms of neurochemicals like cortisol and adrenaline. What is of interest to us is what happens even before the changes in these neurochemicals are detected, and for that we must look at the bioenergy field. In other words, the instant entrainment to the frequency causes a shift in the energy field, which then filters to the physical and biochemical.

During a surgical procedure, I requested that I be allowed to hear the relaxing track of the *Music of Light* on a loop throughout the surgery. After I explained my work and why this was of interest to me both personally and professionally, both the surgeon and anesthesiologist agreed. When I awakened, the music was still playing, and I was extremely relaxed yet alert, without postanesthesia confusion. I was informed that there had been minimal bleeding, and my recovery, which often takes weeks for this procedure, was almost complete within days. I never used the painkillers that had been prescribed.

Was my rapid and easy recovery due to other factors or to my body's relaxation through entraining that affected the bioenergy field? Clearly, this was not a scientific experiment but an empirical one. I can only consider what the doctors said about the usual process of the surgery and recovery and how mine differed. Only with time, research, and appropriate measuring instruments will we be able to document and replicate this sort of experience.

Below you can get a feeling for the spectrum in the *Music of Light* and how each frequency spectrum affects the body. Keep in mind that the colors listed refer to the frequency and vibration that are being transmitted in that particular range, which are then harmonically correlated with music.

Vitalizing (red-orange-amber): increases physical vigor; encourages feelings of vibrant health and well-being; strengthens, invigorates, and energizes; eliminates fatigue and muscle weakness; and stimulates the life-force. It can be as effective as a strong cup of coffee for a pick-me-up!

Tuning (yellow-green-gold): heightens sensory awareness and stimulates efficiency of the nervous system to improve coordination, balance, and reaction time. It causes Alpha brain state to enhance creativity, problem-solving, and concentration.

Relaxing (blue-violet-mauve): increases relaxation and calming; decreases physical and emotional tension; and enhances feelings of wholeness, comfort, peacefulness, and tranquility. As a young child, my son sometimes requested this track of music while he was falling asleep. I recommend it to my patients who suffer from anxiety and mild insomnia. It is also quite calming during the stress of travel, and I have often used it on a loop for sleep during very long overseas flights.

Elevating (blue-white-gold): stimulates higher awareness, peace, and contentment, a sense of unity, and clearer thinking and facilitates processing of problems at a higher level of consciousness and access to more wisdom. It enhances feelings of spirituality and lovingness and can enhance meditation.

Stabilizing (the rainbow spectrum that is a compilation or medley of all the levels): a nourishing, coherent vibrational field that can lead to a feeling of groundedness and a more complete and stable state of being. It can also offset ambient or environmental electromagnetic vibrations that may be confusing and disruptive.

Advancing her discoveries with the *Music of Light*, Valerie Hunt envisioned and developed a prototype for another instrument that used the sound waves audibly or inaudibly; its function was to instruct the body cells in adjusting to a specific combination of frequencies, thus allowing for optimal calibration to counteract certain disease states. With this instrument, a transmitting wire is placed under a sheet in the bed. The color spectrum that is specific for affecting a defined pathology, such as cancer, arthritis, and other disorders, is played on a continuous loop during sleep. Because the important factor is the vibration, this can be generated without audible sound. This instrument, which Dr. Hunt initially called "the vibe grabber," was in its rudimentary stages of development, and only a prototype was made by the end of her life. Again, the development and research will need to be continued by others.

Brain Wave Frequencies for Healing

Other ways of using frequency sounds in healing are emerging. These are related to brain wave frequencies rather than chakra frequencies and merit discussion here as we talk about using bioenergy frequencies for healing. One of the early pioneers in exploring the use of brain wave frequencies, sound, and healing was Robert Monroe, who dedicated himself to the investigation of human consciousness. Using his knowledge from working in radio, he invented the Hemi-Sync® audio technology and founded The Monroe Institute®. Monroe's interest grew from research conducted by a Prussian physicist and meteorologist, H. W. Dove, who in 1838 discovered that when two pure tones of slightly different frequencies are presented, one in each ear, the brain perceives a third "phantom" tone (the wavering sound) referred to as a *binaural beat*.

Gerald Oster, who theorized that the perception of binaural beats could be used as a means of investigating the brain's processes, expanded on Dove's work.[22] Monroe, with this knowledge, started conducting research on the effects of various sound patterns on human consciousness. He documented states of consciousness in which he felt himself separating from his physical body— what he described as an "out-of-body experience." He describes these experiences in his three books: *Journeys Out of the Body*, *Far Journeys*, and *Ultimate Journey*. Eventually he collaborated with other consciousness researchers such as Charles Tart, Russell Targ, Hal Putoff, Stanley Krippner, Stanislav Grof, Edgar Mitchell, and Elisabeth Kubler-Ross, and with professionals such as physicists, electronics engineers, social services executives, psychologists, and counselors to expand on this topic of consciousness.

Although Monroe is best known for his descriptions of his out-of-body experiences, his vision has launched far-reaching levels of applications, best exemplified by Brian Dailey, MD, and Sergey Sorin, MD. These two physicians and researchers, with others, have used the Hemi-Sync® technology in various medical settings, once again demonstrating the power of sound frequencies on the bioenergy field.[23] By using frequencies that correlate to specific brain waves, it is possible for the brain to sync with or entrain to those brain wave states. For example, if you listen to Delta and Theta frequencies, your brain will eventually register something in between, allowing you to sleep or go into deep meditation.

By targeting specific states, this technique has proven effective for insomnia, pre-surgical preparation, intra-operative anesthesia, anxiety, depression, and cancer treatment.[24] In my practice, I have found it a useful adjunct to other treatments. The most dramatic example was with a delightful Korean woman who came to me having experienced her first psychotic break. Since I do not see many patients in my practice with psychosis, I agreed to see her temporarily until she could be established with the county mental health system. When I saw her she was already on antipsychotic medications and medications to counteract the side effects of these antipsychotics, which had been prescribed while she was visiting Korea. She was emotionally very flat, indecisive, confused and, most significantly, tremendously restless and agitated. This restlessness often accompanies the use of antipsychotics, and it was clear to me that this had become an issue for her. Before adjusting medications, thinking that I was only seeing her temporarily, I offered to do Reiki combined with sound medicine (specifically Hemi-Sync® music for relaxation).

As soon as we finished, her agitation and restlessness were reduced and her face, which had appeared almost blank before, had more expression, vividness, and calm. On her follow-up visits, her husband told me that for the most part, this change was sustained at home. I decided to begin tapering her medications to see if we couldn't maintain her free of symptoms. The psychotic symptoms did not resurface and if she felt restless, we again did Reiki, sound medicine, and supportive psychotherapy. After several months she was free of all symptoms and we were able to discontinue her medications completely. It was clear to me that using sound medicine in conjunction with energy techniques had been extremely beneficial in calming her hypersensitive nervous system, allowing her to stabilize.

As our knowledge of bioenergy frequency and frequency sounds becomes richer, sound as medicine has also been gaining acceptance for the treatment and intervention of many health related conditions. Research is mounting to validate its efficacy for use in anxiety, depression, insomnia, pre and post surgery, cancer, and chemotherapy. It is thrilling to realize that there is an emerging range of interventions based on energy that have the potential for treating various medical conditions, for augmenting health, and for strengthening the mind and body. These interventions are less invasive, less intrusive on the natural process, and carry less risk. By appreciating the rudimentary ideas about the human bioenergy field, I hope you are realizing that this potential—your own inherent healing system—is available to you within your own body. Next we will look closer at what goes into creating a smooth flow of energy to continue your path toward understanding your bioenergy field.

CHAPTER 10

PARAMETERS OF THE BIOENERGY FIELD

Coherency and Anticoherency

To understand the bioenergy field and how it plays a part in our well-being, first we need to learn the parameters of the bioenergy field. Parameters are the characteristics, features, and measurable factors that define and identify a particular system. Using her instrument, Dr. Hunt was able to determine that the two most important parameters of the bioenergy field are *frequency* and *coherency*, or flow. Although we have already learned about frequency as it relates to waves, we now want to look at frequency as it applies specifically to the bioenergy field.

Remember that frequency is determined by the number of cycles that occur over an interval of time. The highest frequencies occur during altered states, high consciousness, and spiritual contemplations. The middle frequencies are connected with material problem-solving. The lower frequencies occur with grounding, connection to the physical, and tissue health. There needs to be a smooth flow of energy reflected by the presence of these frequencies in order to be grounded, healthy, attentive, creative, intuitive, and spiritual.

There is a misunderstanding that it is most desirable to be at high frequencies in order to be spiritual. Although higher frequencies are the opening to spiritual experience, it is equally important to have strong lower frequencies. In other words, it is wonderful to be a strong intuitive and connected to the divine (strong higher chakra frequency), but go for a walk, lift some weights, and get mad once in a while (strong lower chakra frequency) while you are at it!

The bioenergy field generates waves. A strong or powerful field is defined by amplitude since it is a measure of force. You might be led to believe this makes for a more coherent field. However, waves can be low frequency with high amplitude in a field or high frequency with low amplitude in a field, and either one can be *coherent*. To understand coherency, let's first look at flow.

Flow means movement with a steady or continual change of one place to another among whatever is being moved. The flow of energy is generated both by the atoms spinning inside the body and from the field outside the body so that there is a continual movement of the particles of the atoms. Flow can be in and out, up and down. It can be coherent or anticoherent.

Coherency means that the flow of energy is consistent in direction, amplitude, or phase; in other words, everything works together and harmoniously. Coherency is present when there is smooth, unblocked flow of energy. That only happens when all the atoms receive the same instruction or stimulus and spin the same in all the cells, all the tissues, all the organs. For example, let's say we have a group of people standing in a room. We tell one person to twirl to the right and another to twirl to the left. Then we instruct another person to twirl while hopping up and down on one foot and the person next to them to twirl around while walking forward. We tell yet another person to twirl around while walking backwards and still another to twirl while walking sideways, and so on. You can imagine what the room would look like. If we try to get something done, it would be hard to do so. If everyone is given the same instruction and moves in the same way, that is coherency.

The chaotic room full of people with opposing direction is

anticoherency—the opposite of coherency. Anticoherency is present when atoms spin irregularly, intermittently, or unequally, or not at all in cells, tissues, and organs, thus creating irregular, intermittent, or unequal flow of energy, or none at all. When some atoms in an organ receive intermittent or irregular instructions, the resulting confusion generates anticoherency inside the body.

Think of a command post where everything is in chaos and no one knows quite what to do. The situation becomes "Every man for himself!" There is no efficiency or efficacy of function. The same thing happens when there is chaotic instruction from the environment to the atoms, cells, tissues, or organs of the body; they receive mixed signals to their spin. The result is a pattern of anticoherency in the field.

Anticoherency can be caused by and manifest as physical pain, strong emotions, and trauma—whether small or large. Sometimes the result of anticoherency is temporary, e.g., stomach pain from food poisoning or the immediate crisis resulting from a car accident. Sometimes anticoherency remains persistent. In the presence of serious physical conditions or severe emotional trauma, such as rape, there may be a persistent anticoherency in the area of the trauma until a resolution is experienced to allow the field to return to coherency. With emotional trauma, resolution means getting to the source and working through the suppressed or blocked emotions. The urgency to resolve internal chaos or anticoherency pushes us into the mind-field, which we will cover in great detail in the last part of this book.

Coherency is a measure of smooth, unblocked flow of energy that happens only when there is strong low, middle, and high frequency. Each person's emotional response determines the nature of these parameters. However, this flow can be blocked or disturbed. Disturbance, similar to the trauma and crises mentioned above, can have a significant effect on the bioenergy field; therefore, coherency relates to the disease or the well-being of the body and mind. Without coherency, in a state of "every man for himself," the body's systems do not work in harmony. If your field is flowing anticoherently, it can lead you to have an immune system that is inefficient or fighting itself and causing diseases, and delayed healing of bodily stresses, strains, and injuries. A lack of coherency can lead you to have a limited range of behavioral responses in solving problems. It can lead to a limited and restricted capacity for happy and successful social interaction. With little or no coherency you may have a limited capacity to be creative in life, blocking art and imagination. And finally, the lack of coherency can result in a blocked capacity for spiritual insights with the inability to use divine power to fulfill your life's destiny.

A Hypothesis about Energy Flow and Disease

Clearly, it is important to achieve coherency. To do so, we need to know what makes the flow of energy anticoherent. Toward the end of her life, Dr. Hunt was developing a very interesting hypothesis related to coherency and disease states. The most significant component of this hypothesis was that specific areas of blockage resulting in anticoherency also caused significant specific pathological conditions.[25] Doing research in cancer with various oncologists, cancer clinics, and patients, combined with substantiated alternative and complementary medicine theories, she determined that weak low frequencies (the lower chakras) were always present in people who developed cancer. By reviewing the fields of numerous patients, she could see a strong correlation when there were very weak low-frequency areas, even when the high-frequency areas (higher chakras) were strong. Conversely, she noted that people who tend to have strong low frequencies but weak high frequencies were more prone to diseases related to cardiovascular phenomena.

Recognizing that low-frequency areas are related to the life-force energy while high-frequency areas are related to more spiritual, mystical energy, she went as far as connecting emotional states with these blockages and the development of anticoherency. This information led her to surmise that it would be possible to create an instrument—the prototype "vibe grabber" mentioned in Chapter 9—that used the frequencies she had previously recorded to entrain the body to strengthen the frequencies in the areas that were weak. An instrument like this would no doubt be a stunning addition for the diagnosis and treatment of cancer as well as other diseases.

Reading the Bioenergy Field with a Pendulum

Even without the availability of a sophisticated instrument, it is still possible for anyone to read the bioenergy field and gain information. One simple way to do so is by using a pendulum. A pendulum is defined as a weight suspended from a pivot so that it is able to swing freely. It will move when there is a force acting upon it. Most often this force is gravity. However, any force, including an electrical or magnetic one, will cause a pendulum to be displaced from its resting position. You have already learned that every energy system has a positive and negative charge generated by the atoms when they spin. Remember that when these electrical charges move, they also produce a magnetic field. The field is not just an electrical one; it is a magnetic one—an electromagnetic field. When the *negative* charge is equal to or more than the positive, the *electrical* force is equal to or greater than the magnetic, allowing for a good flow of energy. When the *positive* charge is greater than the negative, the *magnetic* force is greater than the electrical, indicating a disturbance in the body that disrupts the energy flow.

Using a pendulum, it is possible to get a reading of which forces are present and thus be able to "read" the bioenergy field. When there is a flow of energy (electrical force is greater than magnetic), the pendulum moves in a circular clockwise direction. When the energy is disturbed (magnetic force is greater than electrical), the pendulum moves back and forth. When there is no flow or a very weak one, the pendulum stays still. The movement of the pendulum reflects the presence of the electrical and magnetic forces and their relative strength.

The scientific knowledge base currently available may still question the accuracy of the pendulum, and I recognize that some of this information is based on observations and deductive or inductive reasoning. However, just as we know that dreams can be used as therapeutic tools even though their therapeutic efficacy is based more on deductive or inductive reasoning rather than scientific evidence, so can information derived from the bioenergy field and the mind-field serve as valuable therapeutic tools.

Before the invention of the stethoscope, the doctor put his ear to the patient's chest. Before the electrocardiogram, the doctor had only a stethoscope. So with the potential of more instruments like the Hunt Bioenergy Field Meter, our sophistication in obtaining information about the bioenergy field and the mind-field will improve. In the meantime, we need to use the methods we have available, including the use of kinesiology and the pendulum. In the exercises that follow, you will learn how to use a pendulum to read the bioenergy field.

EXERCISES FOR YOUR BIOENERGY FIELD

Getting Information from the Bioenergy Field

Using a Pendulum

To get information on the flow in the bioenergy field, you will need a pendulum. Keep in mind that here you are not testing for yes or no answers. You are reading the functioning of the bioenergy field according to how the pendulum behaves. A commonly used pendulum is a crystal on a chain, thread, or ribbon. But the simplest pendulum to use is one you can readily make. You will need a weight suspended by a thread or chain. The simplest weight to use is a metal washer (disk-shaped, thin metal plates with a hole in the middle). Tie a length of dental floss through the center of the washer, and you will have your own makeshift pendulum!

Until you are adept at reading the bioenergy field, it is best if the person who is being evaluated is lying down. "Anchor" yourself by being in physical contact with the person. You can do this simply by keeping your hand lightly on the person's leg or arm. This prevents the energy being read from being confused with your own. Settle your own body and mind by getting as relaxed and open as you can be.

You will be testing at the feet, the knees, the seven energy centers (chakras), and the shoulders. As you test, the pendulum will commonly behave in one of three ways: (1) it will move in a circle, usually clockwise (2) it will move back and forth, or (3) it will not move at all. A circular clockwise spin generally means an open field, one where energy is flowing. A back-and-forth movement indicates a stressed field where there is some energy movement, but not completely opened. No movement indicates the field is blocked, and there is no flow of energy. Although I have not seen it often, a pendulum could spin counterclockwise. There is little agreement on what this indicates, but in terms of ease of flow, it probably reflects chaotic anticoherency.

At the feet, knees, and shoulders, an open field will cause the pendulum to move in a circular motion clockwise on the left and counterclockwise on the right. Think of a palm tree with the trunk of the tree representing the spine and the fronds that branch outward from it representing the energy that flows. On the right side of the body, the pendulum spins counterclockwise, and on the left, clockwise.

At the seven energy centers, an open field is one where the spin of the pendulum is a circular movement in a clockwise direction.

Steps to Read the Bioenergy Field

1. Ask the person being evaluated to lie down and anchor yourself to them by being in physical contact.

2. Begin at the feet. Hold the pendulum near the sole of each foot and note what it does. Does it spin in a circular motion (open), spin back and forth (stressed), or remain still and unmoving (blocked)?

3. Next test the knees.

4. Finally, test the seven energy centers.

   • The first energy center is located between the legs and can be read by suspending the pendulum above that area.

   • The second energy center is read by holding the pendulum above the pubis.

   • The third energy center is located just above the navel.

- The fourth energy center is just left of the sternum, between the center of the chest and the left side where the heart is.

- The fifth energy center is at the throat.

- The sixth energy center is in the space between the two eyebrows (the "third eye").

- The seventh energy center is at the top of the head.

As you test each center, note how the pendulum moves.

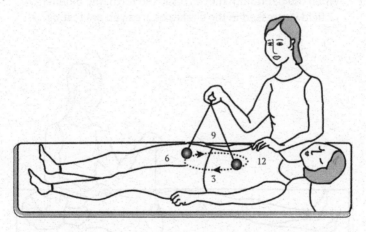

When the pendulum moves in a clockwise direction, the bioenergy field is open in the chakra or area you are testing.

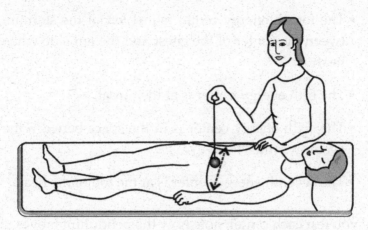

When the pendulum moves back and forth, the bioenergy
field is stressed in the chakra or area you are testing.

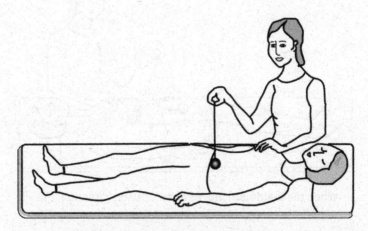

When the pendulum does not move, the bioenergy field is blocked
in the chakra you are testing, and there is no energy moving at all.

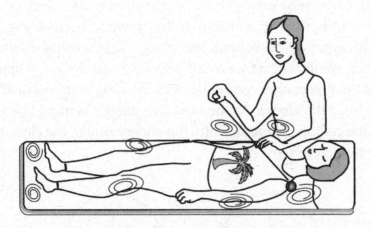

At the shoulders, elbows, knees, and soles, the pendulum moves in a clockwise direction on the left and a counterclockwise on the right, following the pattern of the fronds of a palm tree.

How to Calibrate the Bioenergy Field

Once you know how to read the bioenergy field, you can learn how to calibrate it. *Calibrating* the field means correcting it—bringing it into balance or purposely opening and increasing the flow of energy, at least temporarily. You can do this for yourself or for a person whose field you have read. It is a method of bringing the field into open flow. To learn how to calibrate the field, it is best to begin by lying down on your back, but when you get comfortable with the procedure, you can do it in any position. Calibrating the field will allow you to get grounded, to improve the flow of energy, and to facilitate opening the mind. It is an exercise you can do first thing in the morning, before sleep, or any time you feel anxious, challenged, or need to relax.

You will be visualizing a vortex of energy at each energy center (chakra) spinning clockwise. Visualize yourself *behind* a clock, looking at it from the back, toward its face. You may be tempted to make this easier by saying that you are spinning counterclockwise, but it is important to realize that the spinning is clockwise, and your orientation is behind the clock. This avoids confusion between identifying a true counterclockwise or clockwise spin.

At the first energy center, the clock is facing your feet (and you are behind the clock). At the next five energy centers, the clock faces the ceiling. At the seventh, top energy center, the clock faces away from your feet.

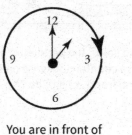 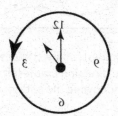

You are in front of   You are in back of
the clock   the clock

Inhale and exhale with the intention of feeling the energy moving through your body. This will increase the flow of energy through each center and will increase the flow of energy in the bioenergy field.

Steps to Calibrate the Bioenergy Field

1. Lie down in a comfortable position and close your eyes.

2. Begin by getting grounded. Take a deep breath and inhale it through the bottom of your left foot. Push that breath up your left leg to your belly and across the back to your hips. Keep moving the breath to the right side and exhale it down the right leg and out the bottom of your right foot. Repeat

this several times until you have established a circuit or a comfortable loop that feels sustained.

3. Take a breath in through the knees and push the breath up to your belly and exhale through your knees. Repeat this several times until you have established a circuit or a comfortable loop that feels sustained.

4. Next take a breath in and out each successive energy center or chakra. Begin at the space between your legs (root), then the pubis (kundalini), the space just above your navel (solar plexus), the area just left of the center of your chest (heart), your throat, the space between your eyebrows (the third eye), and from the top of your head (crown).

Now you are ready to spin each chakra or energy center by visualizing it as a funnel or vortex with the narrow, pointed end toward the spine and whirling outward, with the wider end toward the surface of the body. By this spinning you are strengthening the frequency of energy at each center.

Steps to Spin the Energy

1. Begin with the first vortex at the root. This is the space between your legs. Visualize this vortex in the color red. The direction of the spin is from the top of the pubis, to the left hip, to the tailbone, to the right hip, and back to the pubis. Keep spinning until the red is vibrant in color and there is a consistent circular movement of energy.

2. Spin the second vortex (the kundalini) by visualizing it directly above the pubis. The direction is from the top of the pubis to below the navel, to the left side, to the bottom of the pubis, to the right side, and back to the top. Visualize this vortex spinning in the color orange. Keep spinning

until the orange is vibrant and there is a consistent circular movement of energy.

3. Spin the third vortex (the solar plexus) by visualizing it just above the navel. The direction is from the top of the navel, to the left side, to the bottom of the navel, to the right side, and back to the top. The color is a bright yellow. Keep spinning until the yellow is vibrant and there is a consistent circular movement of energy.

4. Spin the fourth vortex at the heart. The direction is from the top of the chest to the left side, to the bottom, to the right side, and then back to the top. This will be in the color green—a bright spring green. Keep spinning until the green is vibrant and there is a consistent circular movement of energy.

5. Spin the fifth vortex at the throat. Again, the direction is from the top, to the left, to the bottom, then to the right, and finishing at the top. This is in a sky-blue color. Keep spinning until the blue is vibrant and there is a consistent circular movement of energy.

6. Spin the sixth vortex (the third eye) in the space between your brows. The direction is from the top, to the left, bottom, to the right, and finishing at the top. The color is lavender or violet. Keep spinning until the lavender is vibrant and there is a consistent circular movement of energy.

7. The last vortex of energy is at the top of the head (the crown). The direction of the spin is from the top of the head, to the right ear, to the base of the head, to the left ear, and then back to the top of the head. The color is brilliant white. Keep spinning until the white is vibrant and there is a consistent circular movement of energy.

8. Revisit each center, making sure that the spin is still circular, consistent, and in the color it should be. When you get to the top of the head, take the color white and push it down the spine, picking up the lavender, the blue, green, yellow, orange, and red. Now push all this energy out the bottoms of your feet and loop it back to the top of your head, surrounding yourself all around with this color energy as if it were a rainbow of light making an eggshell or cocoon around you.

9. Lie quietly, letting the energy flow and surround you.

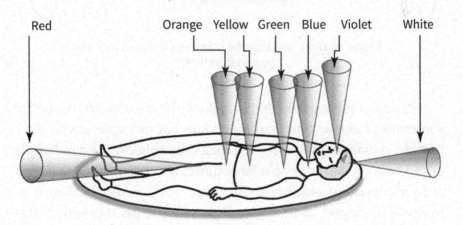

Visualize each chakra spinning in its specific color.

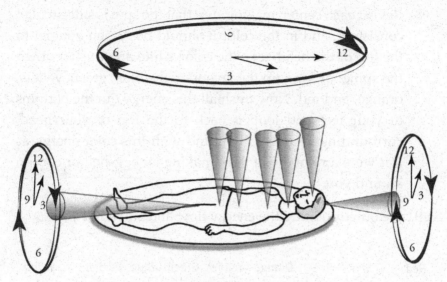

To spin chakras, visualize the spinning clockwise with you
behind the clock.

Should you have trouble visualizing the color at first, visualize
something familiar that is in that color. For example, if you have
trouble visualizing the color red, begin by thinking of a red apple
or red balloon. Some people have difficulty visualizing a spin that
is in a consistent clockwise direction. They may visualize it as
irregularly shaped, or they may feel unable to get it to spin. If this
happens to you, and you think it is an uncontrollable process, ask
yourself, "Who's in charge? Who is directing the spin?" When this
happens in a session, this is the question I pose. The person will
often realize that the feeling "I am not in control" is an illusion and
simply not true. There may be other reasons that a person may
resist allowing the energy to flow openly. Should this happen to
you, be as persistent as possible; try taking charge, and if all else
fails, be forgiving of yourself and wait for another opportunity.

Self-Healing with Bioscalar Energy[26]

Waves have direction based upon their beginning—their source of energy and its location. If you recall, electromagnetic waves radiate from the atoms in all the tissues of our body. As these waves radiate away, they have their own organized electromagnetic field that interacts with other atomic electromagnetic fields. When there are two of these waves, each equal but originating from opposing directions, they flow toward each other. As they meet in the middle, they take on a different direction or frequency. In the middle, they offset and cancel each other's frequencies; they will cause no more frequencies or movement in any direction. As the energies from the two waves have nowhere to go, they become enfolded. This creates an accumulation of the same energy and leaves only standing, dynamic, non-directional (*scalar*) energy, or zero energy.

This energy continues to build up as long as the two waves continue to come toward each other. These are called *scalar* waves, or, because they are occurring in the bioenergy field, *bioscalar* waves. This enhanced energy has the capacity to slowly expand outward in all directions, like water on a paper towel when the surface bonds get weaker. It nourishes and activates atoms in cells to create electromagnetic energy that can heal pain, reduce inflammation, and strengthen tissues.

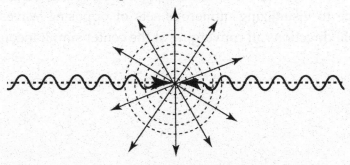

It is your mind that gives the energy the direction and information needed for how to use that standing energy. Wherever there is pain, discomfort, disturbance, or disease, the energy can be brought in from the opposing sides to where it is needed. As the energy builds up, it will expand, moving outward, and then it can be directed to heal the body.

The body knows how to heal itself. Do not direct it to "cure cancer," but rather to heal the body, reduce the inflammation, be healthy, full of vitality, and so forth. If you have pain in your neck, bring the energy from both sides of the neck and direct it to heal the pain. To practice, lie down comfortably, stretching out your arms and focusing on your hands. Visualize the energy flowing from your two hands as two waves coming from opposite directions, toward each other, until the energy from the two waves meet in the center of your body, folding and swirling around each other but no longer moving in any direction. Repeat until you feel the fullness of the built-up energy as it expands, moving outward, loosening tight muscles and connective tissues, expanding the cells in between.

Repeat the process several times. You can bring in the energy from the bottom of your feet to the top of your head, from both sides of your hips, or any other opposite directions. With practice you will become adept at directing the energy for self-healing from two waves coming toward each other. Remember that even though you are visualizing energy coming in from two opposite directions, the radiations or waves are actually coming from all directions. As you get comfortable visualizing two waves, you can advance to visualizing numerous sets of opposing waves from multiple directions all converging at the center simultaneously.

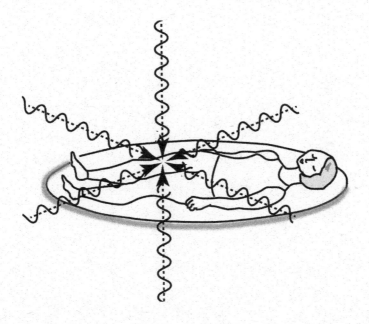

Bioenergy Field Self-Assessment

After you do one of the exercises I have described, I suggest you do the following. Ask yourself these questions, then describe and write your answers as if you were talking to a friend:

- What questions were answered?
- What questions do I still have?
- What did I experience physically?
- What did I experience emotionally?
- What was the hardest part of the exercise?
- What new perspectives and insights have I gained?
- What is the potential for my growth from this experience?

PART III

THE MIND-FIELD, EMOTIONS, BODY, AND SOUL

The terrifying truth about emotion is that unless it gushes and flows freely, it will choke the very soul that creates it. There was never a human that existed in this world that did not yearn to overflow with natural emotion.

—Joshua Loth Leibman

CHAPTER 11

THE BIOENERGY FIELD, MIND, AND EMOTIONS

Up to this point, you have learned a great deal about intuition and the details of the human bioenergy field, but you may be wondering what all this has to do with living an inspired life through expanded self-awareness. With this solid foundation, we are now ready to tackle the more difficult and complex ideas about the human bioenergy field and emotions. Living with expanded self-awareness means living consciously with clarity while taking full responsibility for your life and yourself. The human bioenergy field must be coherent for there to be a consistent sense of well-being, clarity, and openness. If there is anticoherency it is important to identify the source of the anticoherency in order to resolve it.

The most common source of disruption and anticoherency in the human bioenergy field is that of strong, unresolved emotions. Unresolved emotions are held within the mind-field. The mind-field is the information system in the human bioenergy field. Through intensive work to uncover deep-rooted, unresolved emotions, we can identify the source and resolve it. This chapter describes the process of this therapeutic work.

Valerie Hunt first coined the term *mind-field* in relation to the human bioenergy field. The bioenergy field is a filter that screens everything that comes in. It determines how and to what we respond in the world of physical, social, and cosmic happenings. Dr. Hunt described the mind-field as an aspect of the bioenergy field which holds information. The differentiation between mind-field and bioenergy field is essentially an arbitrary one, and the two terms may be interchangeable. Remember that the mind is not an anatomical structure that can be pinpointed. It is a field of information. For our purposes we can think of the human bioenergy field—where we see, hear, and record—as the physical manifestation of the subtler energy of the mind-field—where we experience, feel, and remember. The important thing to keep in mind is that the field—our bioenergy field and mind-field, along with emotions—deeply affects who we are, how healthy we are, and how we live our lives.

The outside edge of the human bioenergy field is what makes contact with our surroundings and the universe. It is the bioenergy field and the mind-field that act as a filtering system and determine the flow of energy—whether that flow revs up, shuts down, lessens, heightens, or is blocked.

These fields are where *transactions* first occur and are recorded. The character of transactions, or how and to what we choose to pay attention, is determined by our emotions. The fields are organized by biology, which stimulates the nervous system, but more importantly, their structure is determined by emotional experience. The strong emotions that structure the bioenergy-field/mind-field arise from experiences in this life or past (more on past lives in Chapter 17). In order to understand what we mean by the structure of the mind-field, we have to understand how emotions, experiences, and the energy created are related.

Definitions

The definitions below are not meant to definitely characterize the components named, but they may help to differentiate the terms I use so you can have a way of conceptualizing the differences.

The *brain* is an anatomical, physical structure composed of cells and nerve connections. This is where information is stored.

The *mind* is not an anatomical structure, but it may be what holds and retains the sum total of all the information that is sent to the brain for recording.

The *bioenergy field* is a human electrical field formed by the spinning of positive and negative ions (as described in the previous chapters). It is where information or stimuli are first received and where transactions first occur.

The *mind-field* is a field related to the mind and may be a refined, more subtle aspect of the bioenergy field. It holds, stores, and integrates information that is to and from the mind. It is not just related to the individual consciousness but to a universal intelligence as well.

The *soul* is the highest level of consciousness that retains integrity throughout one's life and perhaps even past lives. It is unknown whether the soul is part of the mind or whether it is in fact the mind-field.

To understand how all these terms are related, think of a computer. The bioenergy field and mind-field are software. Software is defined as related data or combinations of programs that instruct a computer on what to do and how to do it, and refers to programs and data that are stored in a computer. In other words, software is concerned with the operation of the system. The brain is the hardware, which is the physical, material component of the information system. The soul is akin to cyberspace or the conceptualized "cloud" without a physical correlate. Information is stored in "packets" (or in the language of physics, *quanta*), and can be accessed by any hardware. In other words, what maintains integrity and persists over time, after death, and into other lifetimes are these "packets" (quanta) of information.

Even though I have delineated these structures through the

definitions given, I have done so only for beginning purposes. There are a few qualifiers to keep in mind. The first is that these definitions are simplistic. The reality is probably more complex and fluid. The second is that there is increasing evidence that the bioenergy field and the mind-field are subject to quantum theory, and as such there is a certain degree of unpredictability and inconsistency, making it more difficult to define what these fields really are.

The third is that the soul, for our purposes, is not defined with any religious connotations in mind. It is, of course, the most elusive to comprehend since there is, within the word, a certain element of the unexplainable, or what I call "the mystery." When we delve into this level of exploration, we are going to encounter the mystery, just as many physicists, scientists, philosophers, and thinkers have done. Like all human beings, we can choose to accept the mystery or not. In accepting the mystery, my intention becomes not to attempt to provide all the answers, but to take it as deeply as we can understand, with the purpose of finding ways to live life in the richest, most robust way and to our fullest capacity. Having said this, I will include information that relates to the mystery, in order to push us to the very edge in our exploration of the deepest self and expanded self-awareness.

The foundation you now have will help you understand the critical role that emotions play in developing and maintaining health and well-being. In the chapters that follow, we will delve deeper into the importance of emotions, how they affect the bioenergy field, and the flow of energy.

CHAPTER 12

THE ENERGY OF EMOTIONS

Actions of Energy and Transactions

Emotions are energies stimulated by what we experience in the world, and it is these emotions that structure the bioenergy field. To make sense of this concept, we will start by looking at how energy acts. When talking about fields, we are discussing, at least in part, the physics of energy. When energies meet, one of three things can happen: a reaction, an interaction, or a transaction.

A *reaction* occurs when two physical or mechanical energies come together. In a reaction, there is always one greater energy or force that overwhelms the other. The greater energy is a predictable energy, is constant, and is not a field but a force. The best example of a reaction is to imagine that you are walking along and suddenly trip on a rock. You are most likely going to fall to the ground. At the moment you being to fall, the two energies that have come together are yourself and gravity. Gravity is the stronger energy, so it will prevail, overpowering you, and down you go! This will happen every time such a scenario occurs. It is predictable.

An *interaction* is when chemical or fluid energies come together, affecting one another, and both are changed as a result. Just as its name implies, interactions are actions that occur between two energies to create something different. In an interaction, two energies create a third. Think of two hydrogen atoms and one oxygen atom coming together. They interact and create H_2O, water. Consider what happens when you take blue paint and mix it with red paint; the resulting interaction makes purple paint. In both situations, two or more objects have an effect upon one another, creating a third.

Transactions, as the name implies, occur when an energy goes *trans* or across, beyond, or through to another. Since the energy that goes across is determined by choice (remember, there is a filtering system), energy transactions can only occur between living bioenergy fields. These are dynamic and unpredictable. Each person's bioenergy field actively selects and alters the information it receives. In other words, it *transacts* with stimuli by choice, allowing only *selected* stimuli to come across, or through, from another field. Nonliving fields can react or interact, but not transact. Living bioenergy fields can react and interact *and* transact.

How do we go about choosing what we will transact with? Emotions in our field determine these choices, so transactions are determined by emotions. There can be an interaction between two people, but the effect will be changing and unpredictable, determined by the selectivity of the transaction. In a transaction, the bioenergy field selects what information in the world it wants to allow in. Remember, a transaction means choice, and the choice is determined by emotions. To make this clearer, let's look at some examples.

Let's say you run into Rex. You are feeling just fine and minding your own business. Rex is mad, fuming, and when he sees you, he clenches his fist, curses at you, and lets all that anger out on you. At this point, you (your bioenergy field) has a choice. You can choose how you will transact emotionally with Rex or if you will transact at all. This choice is based on how your field is organized emotionally, or how you are "programmed" to respond to anger. This process is most likely not a very conscious one. Often the effect of the emotions in your field is unconscious until you begin to question why you respond the way you do—in other words, until you become more self-aware.

When you run into Rex, your response will be based on what is in your field. If you have your own anger issues, you may exaggerate his response, become angry yourself or turn that anger inward, wonder what is wrong with you, or even feel depressed. You may dull the response by feeling annoyed, by rationalizing or making excuses for Rex. You may just block anything coming in, like a brick wall, or numb out and not let yourself feel anything. Or if anger does not have that "trigger" in your field, you may just look at angry Rex, shrug your shoulders, think, "What's with him? Must be having a bad day," and continue, unfazed, on your way. In other words, you may choose to not act at all. Or you may be able to transact with Rex in a way that is beneficial to both of you: for example, compassionately, by realizing Rex's anger is not about you but about Rex. Or it may just depend on the other stimuli in your field, so that one time you may respond one way and another time may be different—unpredictable and changing.

The energy field changes and is dynamic depending on the way information is filtered or taken in, meaning according to the transaction. A transaction is about how you uniquely filter information coming into your energy field. It can occur when you are taking in any outside information. How you filter, interpret, or respond will depend on what is in your field. For example, imagine that you and your friend are at the movies. You start to sob at a particular scene, but your friend is unmoved. Your field is structured differently from your friend's, so how you filter what is coming in will also be different from your friend's filter.

Anything that elicits an emotion is a manifestation of a transaction. Think of the emotion in the field as if it were a splinter. The emotional splinter, just like a physical one, can be there unnoticed until it is rubbed, causing you to respond when you become aware of it. Seeing a scene of abuse, whether in real life or as a photo, a movie, or even in internal images generated from reading, will elicit an emotional response. What that response is and how intense a response it is will depend on what emotional energy is in your individual field. If you have personal experiences of abuse, the emotions in your field will be different than if you do not. We could say that anyone would respond the same way, that it is a universal human response. There is some truth to that, but if you examine deeper, there will be subtle variations, much like in a Rorschach test where a person's interpretation of inkblots reveals his or her individual, and sometimes idiosyncratic, inner thoughts and ideas.

Most transactions we experience are between two fields, yours and another person's. Keep in mind that you are not the only one filtering the information—the other person is also. Both of your fields have the potential to filter, interpret, or respond and have the potential to be influenced or affected by each other.

For example, you are feeling fine, but your coworker is very angry and says things to you out of that rage. Let's take a closer look at the common choices we could make when we transact in this situation.

Intensified: Even though your coworker's rage has nothing to do with you, it makes you feel angry because you are sensitive to anger (meaning you hold anger issues in your field). This sensitivity to anger makes you take things personally, and you end up feeling depressed or small and powerless. These responses are intensified or exaggerated, and they will be determined by the structure of your field.

Dulled: To lessen the response you have to your coworker's rage, you numb out, leaving you in a flat emotional state.

Blocked: You simply don't let your coworker's rage in. It is like pretending you have no response or allowing yourself to have no awareness of any response. Although you seem oblivious and unfazed because you are essentially ignoring your emotions, yours is not an effective response.

Mutually beneficial: You are able to respond in an understanding and compassionate way to your angry coworker. Your coworker responds by accepting your understanding and apologizes for his taking it out on you. He ends up feeling more settled, and you end up feeling better as well. The choices made in this transaction settled both of your fields and resulted in being mutually beneficial.

Filter with awareness: When you have great clarity and know yourself well, when you are grounded and have consciousness about who you are, the choices you make in a transaction will reflect this expanded self-awareness. You are free to respond in a way that does not throw you into emotional chaos. You can choose not to engage in another person's drama, especially if you know that it will be a useless endeavor. It is an ideal state in that you can have compassion or walk away, and either way your field stays constant, coherent, and stable.

Notice in the illustration that follows how these transactional choices may play out. Keep in mind that this is a simplified cartoon version to illustrate how a field can be changed and affected.

Choices in a Transaction

Again, understand that this is only a simplified illustration of some of the choices we have in a transaction. To get to know your own transactional responses fully—to get clues as to how you transact—pay attention to your own responses when you see real human images or circumstances and engage in real situations.

Up until now, we have been exploring how emotions manifest based on how they are held in the bioenergy field and the mind-field. In the chapters that follow, we will look deeper at what emotions are, how they become blocked in the bioenergy field and the mind-field, what effect blockages have, and what to do about blocked emotions.

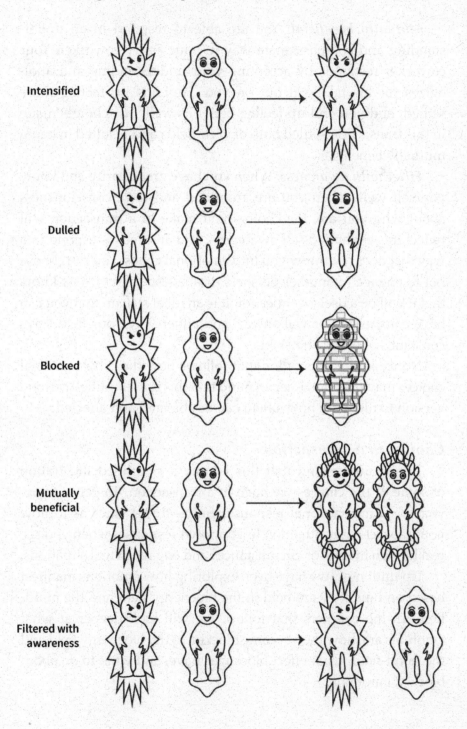

Intensified

Dulled

Blocked

Mutually beneficial

Filtered with awareness

Atoms and Emotions

According to the *New Oxford American Dictionary*, the definition of emotion is "a very intense feeling, which often involves a physical as well as a mental response and implies outward expression." Dr. Valerie Hunt offers an expansion of that in her definition of emotion: "Emotion is an aroused energy that takes a direction. Emotional energy is released whenever there is action. It motivates us."[27] Simplified, she says that emotions are "a power energy source which determines an action"[28] With these definitions serving as a foundation, we can delve deeper into what emotions are, what they do, and how they influence our behavior and the choices we make in our lives.

Every human being has experienced emotion. Even though sometimes we work very hard to block, ignore, or minimize our emotions, they are nonetheless vital to our existence as human beings. (There may be those who, for physiological reasons, appear unable to experience or to name their emotions, but we cannot say they that they do not have emotions.) Emotions give information to our bodies through the energy they generate. Think about it. When you are frightened you are experiencing an emotion first. That energy sends a message to the body, which responds by releasing chemicals that will determine what actions are taken for preservation. In this way, when our bodies are threatened, emotions protect us from destruction or harm at the material or physical level. It is emotions that influence our feelings, thoughts, and opinions about our reality in both the physical world and the spiritual/mystical realm. Valerie Hunt often said that emotions enhance and elaborate our lives. As such they are the source of the power that gives us life. Emotions do this through their energy.

Emotional energy organizes our bioenergy field/mind-field and protects the field from disintegration or threat at the metaphysical or soul level. This crucial role that emotions and their energy play is covered in depth in this chapter.

Previously, we learned that atoms cannot do anything without stimulus. The nature of the stimulus determines how an atom will spin. That spin may be fast, slow, or intermittent. It is this spinning that creates energy. For human beings, life itself is the primary stimulus that causes this spinning. It is the spinning of atoms, and the energy generated, that ultimately leads to the formation, structure, and functioning of the human bioenergy field.

Emotions determine the way an atom spins. Although we know that there is an atomic spin described through quantum mechanics, the existence of this spinning has been only implied by experiments. Observation of its components led to mathematical calculations that are followed by the equations to support the physics. The ultimate source and regulator of the spin has not been fully described in physics.

Valerie Hunt postulated that the strength of emotions could determine how atoms spin. The stronger the emotion, the bigger or faster the spin is, and the greater the energy that is generated. Think about how you feel after you have experienced a great deal of anger. Do you feel exhausted and spent, as if you had just expended a tremendous amount of effort? That is a reflection of the huge amount of energy involved in anger.

Although there are many experiences we call emotions, three basic emotions are the strongest and cause the most powerful spins. The three emotions are anger, fear, and love. These strong emotions are built into the mind-field to protect and enhance life, the body, and soul. Strongest emotions are in the bioenergy field because they are activated during intense experiences, especially when we are unable to handle the powerful emotional energy that arises in response to the experience. Because we are unable to handle that energy, our consciousness is unable to use the experience for learning or for coming to a resolution. Thus, we end up with unfinished business stored in our mind-field, and we develop barriers to remembering or having this information available. In other words, these strong emotional energies are protected by higher consciousness. This process will become clearer in the following chapter as you learn more about the process that occurs in the mind-field as a result of intense and powerful experiences.

CHAPTER 13

THE THREE STRONGEST EMOTIONS

Anger   Fear   Love

Let's look closer at the three strongest emotions. The first is *anger*. The second is *fear*, and the third is *love*. I will cover each in detail and explain why they can be considered the strongest of all emotions.

Anger

The energy of anger is enormous. It arises from the primitive life-force, which will be discussed in more detail when we learn about the kundalini in Chapter 16. With anger, the atoms spin vigorously, generating a huge amount of energy. Think about the last time you were really angry. What did you experience in your body? Did your face get red? Did you sweat? Were you "blinded" by rage? Did your heart race, and all you could think about was lashing out? These feelings are the body manifestations of the energy of anger. They serve to stimulate, to get you going, to do something to get you out of the situation. The energy of anger has the greatest power and is the energy most often repressed. That is why so often we see and talk about misplaced anger. When anger seems to be out of proportion to the causal event, we may wonder if something else is underlying it.

As a psychiatrist and therapist with many years of practice, I have realized that therapy most frequently uncovers anger. In most traditional therapies, the goal is to change anger into something else. Most therapy looks at individual events that have caused or triggered the anger and justifies the response. Often the end goal is an *abreaction* (reliving of a trauma and releasing the repressed emotion) and *catharsis* (an emotional release) related to that singular event or experience. Experiencing catharsis is considered the resolution, and in many ways, it is. There is nothing wrong with this approach. It is valid and an important part of therapy. In some ways, however, it is only a starting point.

For many people, learning to experience the emotion of anger and acknowledging its presence is a beginning essential for recognizing how much it has been blocked. The first step in unblocking emotion is this abreaction and catharsis. For many people, abreaction and catharsis may also be their first experience of paying attention to what they feel and why.

After many years of working in this field, I was never fully satisfied that this level of recognition was enough to truly transform a person's belief systems at the core or deepest level. Such therapy certainly made a dent in resolving the source of the emotion, but often this "resolution" was akin to shaving off a portion of the top of an iceberg, leaving a large portion lurking under the surface. Often people returned with a new version of their distress or a sense that there was more work to do. Sometimes years passed before they realized or felt this need. It is not unusual for me to get a call for an appointment from a patient I have not seen in as many as fourteen years. This may be someone who continues to have or has had a resurgence of symptoms, wants to understand more, feels unresolved emotions still, or is willing to go deeper than before.

This resurgence of symptoms kept me exploring different modalities of therapy and searching for the most effective form of bringing about transformation. It was through my increasing appreciation of the human bioenergy field and the mind-field that I came to see that there might be a deep core source of intense blocked anger that may be found in experiences at the highest level of consciousness. I came to think of blocked experiences and emotions as soul issues, and that these experiences and everything related to them were being held in the mind-field and in the soul.

Fear

The second strongest emotion is *fear*. Fear too has a strong energy. Think about the last time you were afraid. Did you go pale and go cold? Did it feel as if your heart stopped or beat faster? Did your eyes get wide? Did you hold your breath? Did your muscles tense? Did you feel on high alert? These are the body manifestations of fear. Fear serves an important function. It is essential for survival in that it is a protective device. When information is strange or can't be understood or resolved, we experience fear.

The most well-known responses to fear are fight or run, hence the common fight-or-flight response. But there is a third option. This occurs when someone is "paralyzed" by fear. Fear responses can be related to anger. If the fear occurs with *stimulated* anger, it makes us *fight*; this might be considered a hyperactive response. Fear with *repressed* anger makes us *freeze*; this is a hypoactive response. Fear without anger is what makes us run.

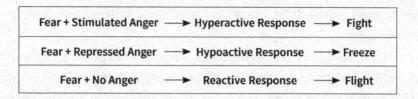

Ultimately the purpose of this increased/hyperactivity or repressed/hypoactivity is to be life preserving, but it can also become life threatening. The energy associated with the emotion of fear is immense and can be exhausting. In psychotherapy, what I have already said about anger applies to fear. Most often it is dealt with at the cognitive-behavioral level, such as through some sort of desensitization or behavior modification. Again, abreaction and catharsis can be very helpful and effective for a time, and it may be all that a particular individual can do, but often it does not really address the deeper source of the fear.

Love

The third basic emotion is *love*. In an interview on the art of living, Roman Krznaric, a cultural thinker and writer, said this about love:

"Ancient Greeks were much more complex in the art of loving. They had one word, *eros*, for sexual love and sexual passion. They had another word, *philia*, for deep comradely friendship. Another word, *pragma*, was about the mature love between long-married couples—about giving love as well as receiving it, and compromise. There was *agape*, their concept of selfless love, which is where we got our word "charity," from *caritas* which was the Latin translation of *agape*. And there was *philautia*, which is self-love—the idea that we need to nurture a healthy self-love. And the sixth kind is *ludos*, playful love."[29]

In one short paragraph, Dr. Krznaric highlighted the most important feature of love—that it is multifaceted and defies a simple definition. What he described about love emphasizes how enigmatic and tricky discussing, much less understanding, love can be. What we can say is that untainted love is a joyful emotion. Unlike anger and fear, love is not primarily protective but rather serves to embellish, enhance, and enrich our lives. It can be experienced in many forms: peaceful, gentle, or expansive, or intense and passionate. Love can be spiritually ecstatic. The experience and sensation of love is pleasurable.

We all feel love, think we feel love, want to be loved, and interpret a whole range of experiences as love. But love experiences can become distorted, accompanied by misinterpretations about what love is, and result in emotional problems. Misperceptions of love or expressions of love can result in feelings of trauma, rejection, and insecurity. Undistorted love has a strong energy that embellishes and enhances the field, while distorted love leads to aberrations in the field that are detrimental and not life enhancing. These distortions, apart from having behavioral consequences, can lead to tissue stress, social dysfunction, and soul trauma or shock.

People who have always had to please others in order to feel loved will believe that they can only have love if they are pleasing someone. Without awareness, these people will continue to blindly try to please, never taking into account their needs and accepting whatever they are given. Ironically, these people may be trying so hard to please others that they lose the capacity to love genuinely because all their energy goes into trying to figure out what to do to be pleasing. This discounts not only their needs, but the person they are trying to please as well. In other words, this futile attempt at pleasing wastes energy. Often these people will develop chronic symptoms such as headaches, pain, and depression. I have seen patients with this dynamic who, when faced with a serious illness such as cancer, realized that they had lived always compromising their own lives—repressing their own urges and desires for the sake of others. This is not to say we should not take into account the needs of others, but rather that we need to be equally mindful of our own, something that comes with expanded self-awareness.

As human beings, we cannot survive, develop, or function optimally without love. That is what makes it one of the three strongest emotions. The closer we come to experiencing un-distorted love, the healthier, the happier, the more conscious, and the more generous we can be in our experience of love. The emotion of love will be that much stronger and vibrant.

Subemotions

When asked to name emotions, many people often include sad-ness, irritation, nervousness, anxiety, frustration, or happiness. However, I have asserted that there are only three major emotions. What are these other experiences that we call "emotions"? All other experiences we call emotions are a variation, dilution, or masked expression of anger, fear, or love. Valerie Hunt referred to these as *affects*. To avoid confusion with the psychological definition of affect, which is "the intensity and range of emotions," I have reconceptualized these experiences as *subemotions*. Think of subemotions as the expressions, projections, or partial manifestations of one of the three basic emotions. For example, anger may not be expressed in its true form as anger but in a diluted form such as annoyance, irritation, frustration, or even depression.

Although people often consider emotions and subemotions to be equal in intensity and power, there is a difference when viewed from the bioenergy perspective in that the strong emotions will generate more energy than the subemotions. Any subemotion, if followed to its source, will ultimately lead to a strong emotion. Most often, the subemotions related to anger are depression, hostility, persecution, frustration, and hate. The subemotions of fear are anxiety, panic, insecurity, guilt, helplessness, and confusion. Finally, the subemotions of love are pleasure, happiness, joy, faith, compassion, and grief.

Grief is a difficult emotional experience to categorize. All grief is about loss, and how grief manifests will depend on what is lost and the relationship to that which is lost. A patient told me that she thought grief was either selfishness or guilt. Perhaps selfishness or guilt may at times be a component of grief, but ultimately I suspect the most profoundly felt grief is when there is underlying love. For that reason, I include grief as a subemotion of love.

Anger	Fear	Love
Depression	Anxiety	Pleasure
Hostility	Panic	Happiness
Persecution	Helplessness	Joy
Frustration	Insecurity	Faith
Hate	Guilt	Compassion
	Confusion	Grief

There may be some overlap of a subemotion with more than one emotion. Because the energy of the basic emotions is so powerful, it is often more difficult to express the raw emotion acceptably or effectively. Subemotions end up being a way to "leak" this energy more slowly, cautiously, and often more acceptably. The result is that the subemotion can become a chronic state, while the real source of the strong emotion is masked and repressed. Without resolution of the repressed emotion, the energy of the field becomes distorted.

The most common reason emotions become distorted is related

to culture and behavior. All behavior has an emotional component. Experiences that are tragic, stressful, loving, and exciting stimulate the strong basic emotions of anger, fear, and love. These strong emotions create and control the amount and way energy is used to respond and to behave. Only the strong basic emotions determine the pattern of the mind-field.

Emotions are often distorted by culture, and the emotions that are distorted the most and are the most intense and difficult to handle are anger and fear. Love is our favorite. It makes us feel good, and we usually claim it as the one we feel most comfortable with. Often, however, the capacity to experience love is diminished if anger or fear are too distorted or blocked from healthy expression, or if love has been tainted, confused with, or accompanied by anger or fear.

The three emotions and all the attendant subemotions exist within us. We express them either effectively or ineffectively. When emotional energy is flowing freely, emotions are expressed effectively without distortion. When emotional energy is blocked, emotions are usually expressed ineffectively because they become distorted. The next chapter discusses how and where emotional energy becomes blocked from flowing freely, and later chapters describe what can be done to resolve blocked energy.

CHAPTER 14

WHEN EMOTIONS GET BLOCKED

How Emotions Get Blocked

When emotions are distorted and not allowed free expression, they and the energy they generate become blocked and affect the bioenergy field. Each of us has unique experiences with differing emotional responses resulting in our own interpretations and distortions. Because of this, the bioenergy field differs in structure with each individual person, much like a fingerprint. This difference is not just based on biological and physiological factors such as genetics or neurological anatomy/physiology, although these do play a role. The difference arises also from how the bioenergy field is structured by experiences in this life, before birth, in childhood, and even in past lifehoods (a term I will define in more detail in Chapter 17 when I discuss reincarnation). This structure establishes the bioenergy field and brain patterns. In turn, this structure contains and determines the value we place on specific physical, emotional, spiritual, and cosmic sensations. It affects how our physical senses take in light, sound, touch, taste. It regulates how we interpret and respond to the cultural meanings of our personal and global social world. It influences the way we seek and resonate with metaphysical and spiritual experiences.

Emotions are activated during intense experiences when the person is unable to handle the powerful emotional energy that arises. In these situations, the consciousness is unable to use, resolve, or minimize the experience. This unused energy leads to unfinished business, kept in the mind, with barriers to knowing it consciously. Because the emotional energy becomes blocked, emotions also become blocked. An intense, traumatic, or tragic experience in this life or in a past lifehood results in the need to make an urgent decision to change, control, or manage what is happening. Intense and profound emotions go along with these decisions. This urgency and irrationality results in the person making decisions in a state of weakness and with a lack of clarity or insight. In such a situation, the intensity of the emotions with the energy and power generated is so strong that it becomes almost intolerable. The only thing that seems acceptable is to block it all from consciousness. Everything that goes along with the experience, including the experience itself, the reason for the response to it, the emotions, and emotional energy, are blocked and become stuck.

The response becomes unconsciously ingrained in the mind-field. If the response was for the person to become powerless, victimized, helpless, or numb, these feelings are what is retained. Sometimes a person might have wanted to or known they needed to act powerfully, to fight, or to maintain complete clarity and understanding, but in spite of wanting to act, they did not. Both the realization that they knew they had an option of action and the actual decision they made may be what is blocked. A person who is blocked in this way will stay entrenched in the belief system, emotions, and patterns of behavior that they did not allow into their consciousness; this pattern stays hidden, aided by repeating the behaviors and choices. In other words, if a person made urgent, irrational choices that led to feeling victimized and powerless, their response in future challenging situations is more likely to be the repeated one of feeling victimized and powerless.

Whatever the thoughts and behavioral patterns associated with the circumstances and consequences of that decision, they become deeply ingrained in the mind and held as information in the mind-field. The person can access this only with deliberate intention and willingness to become unstuck, but most often behavioral patterns are perpetually repressed, to be triggered in the course of transactions with the world. Like emotional splinters, they are ignored until they are rubbed the wrong way, making them noticeable and uncomfortable.

An example of a blocked emotion would be of a veteran who has experienced war. During the experience, the soldier made decisions without thought to consequences because of continuous life-and-death situations. Sometimes there appeared to be no choices for survival other than extremely difficult ones. Only later do the strong emotions that accompanied this experience begin to arise.

A memory that forces the person to face the consequence of an action may have been hidden or repressed. A future similar situation acts as a trigger for recalling the details of the experience. Triggers are sensations, acts, or events that serve as a stimulus, eliciting a response or reaction. Often they are a type of reminder or reenactment of something that has been consciously suppressed or forgotten. Because the emotions are so deep and so repressed, the behavior and symptoms that are triggered, along with the accompanying panic and other physiologic responses, are now known as Post Traumatic Stress Disorder (PTSD).

All of this is reflected in how energy flows and how it is manifest in the bioenergy field. Strong emotions, therefore, with their energy and information within the field, are the ones that structure the field. Triggers set up a repeating cycle of behavior when it comes to choice of action, thoughts, and responses; I have termed these *pattern dynamics*. Pattern dynamics are carried in past lifehoods and into this life as ingrained patterns of perceptions, beliefs, and behaviors.

Pattern Dynamics

Responding in the same way when faced with similar situations, a pattern is created in the bioenergy field and, over time, becomes embedded from the mind into the brain like a groove in an old-fashioned record or like a well-worn path. These bioenergy-field and brain patterns contain and determine the way we value our experiences in the world—the values we place on our sensations, the cultural meanings of our environment, and our spiritual or mystical beliefs and experiences. The manifestation of the information held in the energy field is called the *pattern dynamic*. Pattern dynamics are the visible cognitive, behavioral, emotional, and psychological reflections of the constructs that are repeated. They determine our belief systems, or what we believe about our capacity, our environment, and ourselves. They determine our responses to the internal and external world and to the events that give us sorrow or pleasure.

Why do we develop these patterns in the field? How do these pattern dynamics get established? Why do we repeat them? To answer these questions, we need to know what the functions of the bioenergy-field patterns and the resulting pattern dynamics are. It seems clear that to have such a strongly ingrained, repetitive dynamic occur, there must have been a powerful intention behind the creation of that dynamic. The most powerful motivation for human beings is to preserve life, and the largest threat to life is from catastrophic physical, emotional, and spiritual experiences. The patterns and the beliefs that fuel them arise from the choices we make at those critical times. (More on the choices we make in life-threatening situations will be covered when we discuss the life-preserving energy surge in Chapter 16.) The reason we develop patterns is to protect our bodies, our selfhoods, and our souls. Especially over time, these patterns give rise to the forces that lead us to experience stagnation, to stay stuck, and to hold us back or give us the stimulation to move toward change.

Since we know that emotions generate energy, it makes sense that extreme emotional situations will generate extreme energy. During major life crises, when the soul and body are threatened, the extreme emotions generated are expressed as a huge surge of energy. The way in which that energy is used or blocked at the time of its first occurrence leads to our thought and behavior patterns, which are designed to protect us by helping us escape the threatening situation. These patterns are recorded in the mind-field to provide for future security. Even if they are not the best choices, they become embedded, and we do the same thing again and again.

Let's say you are faced with a catastrophic or tragic event in life. You need to make a decision about what to do. Most often we face these situations with weakness, insecurity, and a lack of insight. What may seem like the only options at the time are not always the best or wisest choices. The intense emotional power that goes along with these choices causes the pattern to become ingrained, making it seem as if these choices are forever unchangeable.

When we consider what we already know about the mind, the soul, and the information held there, we realize that even if these tragic or catastrophic events occurred in a past life, the pattern dynamic is as present as if it had occurred in this life. In fact, if you have been repeating the same behavior over and over, it can become so strongly entrenched in your entire belief system that it feels impossible to recognize any other option for behavior, thinking, or making choices.

The outcome of the pattern dynamics is that they keep us rigid, limiting our repertoire of responses, our capacity to take in new information, and our creativity. The people who are unwaveringly predictable in how and what they decide to do in decision-making situations may be demonstrating a reflection of this rigidity. Indecisiveness is also a reflection of a pattern dynamic that may have become ingrained from an intense experience; there were so many choices at the time that it was impossible to get focused in the body and mind. This led to confusion and staying stuck. These people cannot seem to make their minds up about anything. Too many choices! Either of these kinds of people, whether rigid or indecisive, will have difficulty being open to new ways of perceiving themselves, others, and the world around them.

How Pattern Dynamics Develop

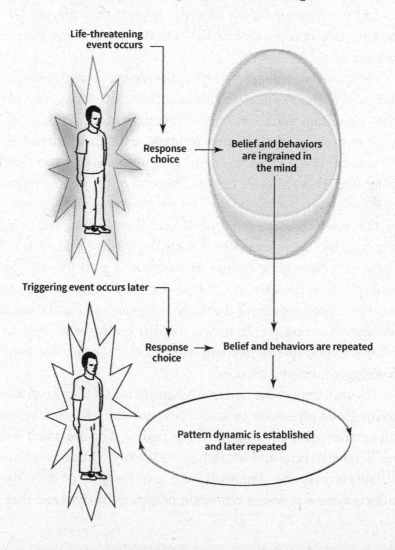

A simplified version of pattern dynamics can be found in the writings of Freud when he writes about the concept of *repetition compulsion*.[30] Repetition compulsion is a defense mechanism whereby a person repeats traumatic or unresolved experiences by recreating them, often unconsciously. This explains why, without even realizing it, a man might marry a woman who has the same characteristics as his mother. The theory is that by duplicating a similar relationship situation, the issues that could not be worked out with the parent can be resolved more successfully with the spouse—a futile attempt to rewrite history. In addition, a sense of familiarity in the relationship dynamics makes it more comfortable. Many times I have encountered patients who were unwilling to change a difficult situation because there was a certain degree of comfort and familiarity to it. Better the devil you know than the devil you don't know, so to speak.

As we go into deeper layers of the psyche, repetition compulsion continues in more complex forms that are more deeply established and more difficult to access. Working with the bioenergy field, the mind, and the energy of emotions, we may now attempt to identify the ultimate source of pattern dynamics and to transform them.

Where Emotions Get Blocked

Let's delve further into where emotions block energy flow and what to do about it. The places where energy flow can be blocked are in the body, the brain, and in our highest consciousness.

The body is the most material, physical, tissue level. Energy flow blocks can be felt by bodywork techniques. Practitioners who rely on their ability to sense the presence of energy flow use interventions that, for the most part, are based on the idea that the body holds or remembers emotional blocks. Most therapies that deal with this—craniosacral/somatoemotional release therapies, healing touch, Reiki, Rolfing, and others—approach the source as emotional trauma that is held in the tissue and this is reflected in the energy flow. When trauma is locked and held in the tissues and in the body, then released when manipulated, emotions may or may not be experienced, expressed, or released. Energy flow can improve through body and energy manipulation. This can be effective for alleviating physical symptoms or stress. There can be relief at a certain level. In some bodywork techniques, a therapist may encourage a client to verbally process emotions that arise as part of the therapy, but for the most part, bodywork does not require an awareness of the source of the emotions.

All bodywork can be relaxing and reassuring, and for some this may be enough, or all that is tolerable. However, if emotions are the source of symptoms or of stress showing up in the body, then these therapies may not be enough. When emotions are not addressed, the body "takes the hit" and, after a time, the problems often recur, sometimes as the same body problems, sometimes as different body issues. For example, a person may have intense unresolved emotions that manifest as jaw pain. The jaw pain may be resolved or improved with bodywork, but then the person may develop an awareness of back pain.

Of course, not all pain and body problems originate with emotions. A person in a car accident will have pain from trauma. Emotions, however, may influence how the person responds to treatment. How a person responds or recurrence of the same or similar symptoms are indicators of deeper layers of unresolved emotions. Similarly, the brain and central nervous system (CNS) and its network of electromagnetic components can develop blocks to energy flow. These occur in areas that have primary control of physiological systems, organs, and even DNA instruction to cells.

Energy flow can improve through methods that require the brain and nervous system to be engaged. These may include artistic expressions such as painting/drawing, music, drama, writing, and storytelling that tap into the emotional energy as well as engage the CNS. Neurolinguistic programming, guided imagery, tai chi/qigong, and meditation can help improve energy flow as well. Improvement can occur in brain functioning, in creativity, and even in insight. But just as with the body, resolution that does not incorporate identifying the source of the emotional block or the deeper layers is most likely to be incomplete.

Highest consciousness blocks are related to tragic experiences in the current life or lifehoods (past lives) leading to trauma at the soul level. Energy flow can improve by activation at the spiritual/mystical level by opening the mind-field with greater coherency, and by returning to the superconscious states that store the memories that are recalled and re-experienced. This results in elevated states that restructure the field.

Valerie Hunt coined the term *life-shock* and developed ways to gain insights that allow for soul-level resolution to take place. In many ways, exploring a life-shock gets the closest to the source of emotional blocks. It is while working at this level that I have witnessed deeper, stronger, and longer-lasting transformations in people who have been willing and ready to face and tolerate this work.

As you can tell, there is overlap between the places—body, brain, higher consciousness—where energy can be blocked. In fact, the blockage of flow at one level affects all the others, as though water was flowing through a series of pipes from a large reservoir. The largest pipe is the one closest to the source where the largest amount of water flows. Connected to it are other pipes, and so on. At any place there can be a blockage, and no matter where that blockage is, it will affect all those connected directly or indirectly to it. In the case of energy flow, none of the three levels alone is complete. The tissue level is too small and localized, the neurological level is too materially focused, and the highest consciousness or soul level is too big and cosmic. The ideal is to recognize that all three are intertwined. It is possible to deal with a specific level when needed. It is appropriate to engage at a specific level according to a person's capacity. Not everyone can begin by finding a resolution to blocks at the level of highest consciousness.

The traditional tools of medicine, body intervention, subtle body-energy work, and spiritual practice all have a place and are there for us to use as needed. When asked about my nontraditional way of doing psychiatry, I often say I have not "thrown out the baby with the bathwater." In the most dramatic example, if you were in the throes of a heart attack, exploring highest consciousness issues would not be timely or appropriate. You should call EMS, take aspirin, go to the ER, and get a stent or even cardiac bypass surgery. Later, when you have survived the immediate crisis, you can explore the highest consciousness to see where the field is not coherent, what caused the body to show disease, and where the emotional blocks are, and then you should find the resolution. But you have to be alive to do that, and for that you will need all the tools and interventions available to you.

Less dramatically, I freely use traditional medicine and medications, especially if someone is not functioning well. What has to come first is physical and mental stabilization. People often come to consult with me thinking they do not want any medications. I respect their choices. At the same time, if I see that they are not functioning well on a day-to-day basis, I will explain the use of medication to them using this analogy: A ring gymnast needs to train, but he has a coach, and one of the functions of the coach is to give the athlete a boost up to reach the rings. Then it is up to the gymnast to do his best. The medication sometimes is just the boost.

Ideally I would never use medications, but the reality is that many people have not reached the point where they are able to do the inner work required because of the demands of their everyday lives. Over time, some people have been able to tackle this work and significantly decrease or discontinue medications. First we stabilize the physical; then we deal with the emotional and spiritual. I am careful not to promise that recognizing the source of energy blocks, releasing them, and resolving them is the be-all and end-all. I often say the body is the body, and sometimes it is difficult to reverse or change physical conditions.

Although I believe we can use our inner power and innate intelligence for healing, it is just not always possible to reach the ideal. If this happens, it is important to avoid blaming yourself and feeling at fault, feeling that you have not taken responsibility for blocked emotions, or feeling guilty for not doing enough work. Whatever degree of awareness and understanding you come to is a step upward. There are some who believe that it is not necessary to do the "heart-wrenching" work of uncovering or working through blocked emotions. I believe it is valuable to gain as much insight and clarity as possible by doing the work and unblocking the energy flow so that the maximum capacity for resolution and transformation can be attained and manifested. Being fully in the process, naming the emotions, knowing them, and feeling and resolving them empowers you by allowing you to take responsibility and own them. Whatever gains in awareness are made will be remembered in the field and will stay with you.

Blocked emotions keep us in shackles. We tend to experience and express them, usually inappropriately, through our distorted filters that underlie them. It is liberating to know your emotions, where they came from, and how they influence you, and with this you can learn to experience increased self-awareness and to express emotions effectively.

CHAPTER 15

LIFE-PRESERVING ENERGY SURGE

Introduction to the Kundalini

In extreme situations, people experience intense emotions leading to a surge of life-preserving energy. This energy is a reflex available to all. It generates tremendous power. It is what allows a person to perform extraordinary feats in dire circumstances. It has been called by many names, which should sound familiar from the previous chapter when we talked about bioenergy: in Chinese, *qi* (*chi*); Hindu: *prana*; Japanese: *ki*; Tibetan: *rLung*, or inner "winds" of life-force; Egyptian: *ka*, or vital essence; Hebrew: *Ruach Ha Kodesh*, for Breath of God; Arabic/Islamic: *Nafs* and *Ruhi*, the terms for a kind of "soul breath"; Latin/Catholic: the Holy Spirit; and even the Force in what has been become the Star Wars mythology.

As a student of tai chi, I learned that the source of power was the dantian, located three finger's-width down from the navel, corresponding anatomically to the kundalini, which corresponds to the second chakra. The Chinese word *dantian* means "life elixir" or energy center. It was fascinating that both the dantian in the Chinese culture and the kundalini in the Hindu culture are located in the lower part of the abdomen, just below the navel, that both are energy centers, and that both store the life-force energy associated with each culture (*qi* in Chinese culture and *prana* in Hindu culture). In both traditions, this energy is related to the source of life, and its tremendous power lies dormant until awareness or need allows for an unleashing, beginning at the base of the spine or the lower abdomen and rising up and out. Since energy is a multidimensional, radiating phenomenon, it is conceivable that the kundalini (described as lying dormant at the base of the spine and often depicted as a coiled snake) refers to the same thing as the dantian (depicted as a furnace lying dormant at the lower part of the belly).[31] Although here I am referring only to the Chinese and Hindu traditions, which are related, there is a striking similarity, cross-culturally, among many groups throughout the world. As we learned earlier, almost all cultures have a concept related to a great source of life that generates energy, available to all. The multicultural similarities make it more difficult to disregard the validity of the existence of this powerful energy that the body is capable of releasing.

In extreme situations, if the life-preserving energy reflex is needed and allowed to rise unfettered, the energy will flow freely (unblocked); this is the energy that stimulates the ability for extraordinary physical, mental, and spiritual responses. How someone handles that surge initially, the very first time it is triggered, is determined by whether it subsequently flows freely or is blocked when needed again. Just as with most reflexes, only two things can happen when that reflex arises. One is that the energy is released, and the other is that the energy is suppressed or blocked. The accompanying emotional energy is also released or blocked. So emotions will determine where and how energy flows.

Blocked emotions can affect the life-force energy and its ability to flow freely and openly. This life-force energy is called the *kundalini*. This is a complex topic, but since it is connected to my method for unblocking emotions from previous lives, I will address it here. The kundalini is a profound surge of energy likened to a coiled snake lying dormant at the base of the spine (first chakra) that, when stimulated or aroused, uncoils and ascends the spine, opens the third eye (sixth chakra) and surges out of the top of the head (seventh chakra). This awakens the consciousness, and immense understanding and insights ensue. The term was first recorded in the Upanishads, ancient Vedic texts, around the eighth century BCE but has been identified in many other traditions and cultures. The word *kundalini* translated from Sanskrit means "coiled" or "the coiled power."[32] There is much about this kundalini energy that is not really understood, but it is clear that it occurs as a real phenomenon and can arise in any human being.

Ways to Understand the Kundalini

In trying to understand the kundalini energy, I decided to differentiate the kundalini experience by three points of view related to the process. The first, most traditional, and perhaps most important, is as a vehicle for enlightenment and conscious awakening; the second is as an inducible physiologic function; and the third is as a spontaneous, life-preserving energy surge. These are arbitrary differences reflecting more how we experience the kundalini than what the kundalini is, since in essence, the kundalini is the same regardless of how it is viewed.

Many mystics, yogis, and seekers of spiritual enlightenment have described kundalini ascension as a consciousness awakening experience attained through a guru, a master, or a spiritual guide. When it occurs, it is a life-altering and mind-altering event, one in which there is a sense of spiritual connectedness and cosmic understanding, devoid of ego or attachment to the physical. The kundalini awakened through spiritual transmission by the grace of a guru or teacher is a process called *shaktipat*. Spiritual practices such as yoga or meditation can also awake the kundalini.

During the arising of the kundalini there can be intense physiological sensations and sensory experiences, vivid images and new understandings. The experience can be ecstatic, with overwhelming visions of the divine, or it can be frightening and disturbing. Various mystics describe this ultimate transcendent experience in different ways. Most often we think of a guru such as Paramahansa Yogananda achieving this awakening, but when we read the writings of the Christian mystic Hildegard von Bingen, or the poems of the Sufi mystic Rumi, and even some Shamanic initiations, they too seem to be describing kundalini awakenings.[33]

This kundalini rising is what I think of as the ultimate awakening. Once it is known, life, perceptions, and beliefs are forever altered. Although many of us may come close to having this degree of awakening, I doubt most of us experience the full-on opening of consciousness. Those who have experienced it can be recognized by the way they live their lives: think of the greatest sages such as Jesus and Buddha, or many others who live without ego, only expressing love and compassion through their actions.

The second point of view is the kundalini as a physiologic process. This is beautifully described in Dr. Joe Dispenza's book *Becoming Supernatural*. Although he is reluctant to refer to the term kundalini, he admits the physiological process he describes is in fact that.[34] It would be an injustice to try to synthesize Dr. Dispenza's elegant description of the physiology and chemistry of the kundalini rising. I have included his book in the references. In essence, with well-documented research, he describes how contracting the muscles associated with the first, second, and third chakras (the perineum and lower and upper abdominal muscles) while deeply inhaling will set in motion a series of physiologic, neural, and chemical reactions. This contraction causes the cerebral spinal fluid to be pushed up the spine, triggering reactions that include stimulating the pineal gland, releasing neurochemicals, and creating Gamma waves in the brain (a state of heightened awareness).

Remember that all physiologic activity is accompanied by energy and this sequence of events has energy that increases in frequency as it ascends until it reaches very high frequency states.

The energy moves out of the body, creating a torus or torsion field and the body draws energy back in. As you recall, this torsion field carries information. The entire process allows for awareness to move from the body to mind. The heightened state of awareness that results then allows for an interface between the bioenergy field/mind-field and what we may call the unified, quantum, or cosmic field. Working in conjunction with what Dr. Dispenza and others call "the greater mind," we can deliberately draw on this field where all possibilities exist to create our reality. It is at this point, disconnected from the physical plane, that we return to the kundalini experience as a mystical, transcendental, or divine experience.

The third point of view of the kundalini is what Valerie Hunt classified as a life-preserving reflex. For her, the kundalini reflex was intricately linked with blocked emotions at the deepest levels. We have learned that intense emotional energy structures the bioenergy and mind-fields. These intense emotions can arise during critical, often life-threatening, events. The most crucial response triggered is the life-preserving energy surge or the kundalini reflex.

In this point of view, it is a universally present physiological response whose sole purpose is preservation—to protect the life and the soul. When there is complete openness and coherence, when energy is flowing well throughout the body, the kundalini energy arising from the base of the spine flows openly and coherently. This acts as a creative, health-inducing, and robust force. Exposed to a serious life-threatening event, the mind accesses great emotions and powerful energies so that the body can handle the shock. As a life-preserving reflex, the kundalini is a part of an intense and immense energy release. This stimulation from the brain to the base of the spinal cord is so powerful that it activates all systems to move intensely fast against any resistance. It is an extraordinary energy, and when it arises in full force, the intensity of the experience and the emotions associated with it are stored as information in the mind and in the bioenergy field. This information is held throughout a lifetime or even through past lives.

This life-preserving energy surge or kundalini reflex is a human reflex and has certain universal characteristics. Once this energy begins to flow, it is accompanied by intense physical sensations beyond a normal surge of adrenaline. Some may feel great heat or great cold, tingling, shaking, electricity, or an inner sense of light shooting from the top of the head. The energetic power released is tremendous and capable of anything in the service of preservation.

We all have heard about extraordinary feats of valor during catastrophic situations. For example, a person may lift a car to save the life of someone pinned underneath. As a life-preserving instinct, it is amoral and without judgment, causing us to protect, even if it means hurting or killing another. It arises out of a human's highest consciousness with the intention of preserving life, to fulfill the soul's destiny. This does not mean the *intention* of the kundalini is to kill or hurt; instead, it is to preserve. Because the kundalini reflex is so powerful, its release is not only life preserving but may also be transcendent, connecting the person and the soul with divine power. It is a manifestation of our most powerful capacity, not only an instinctual need to preserve the body but also guided by inspired insight to preserve the soul. Here is where our previous understandings of the kundalini overlap.

There are those who seek the kundalini reflex and want to activate the intense, transcendent experience through force in order to tap into the mystical states. Others believe the raising of the kundalini occurs through grace, of sorts, and relies on a readiness that cannot be forced. It can be unproductive and even dangerous to force the kundalini to rise. There are people who have had severe physiologic or psychological reactions, and for this reason the practices such as kundalini yoga designed to induce the kundalini rising often have a guru or master to oversee the experience. Inducing the kundalini is not always detrimental, however. For example, Dr. Dispenza has ample data that suggest the mediations he uses to stimulate the kundalini rising have had highly beneficial effects on health, well-being, and spiritual connectedness.

There are probably degrees of activation or partial rising involved when we talk about stimulating the kundalini to rise. I have often heard people describe an "incredible" meditative experience that resulted in the rising of the kundalini. They describe all the elements of the transcendental experience, meaningful to them. I ask how they felt, and often they will describe a sense of wholeness, peace, calm, or even ecstasy. Then I ask how long the experience lasted or how they were transformed. Usually they respond that it lasted for a period of time, but then they reverted to being as they were before, with the same sense of self, beliefs, and consciousness.

Although the experience had some benefit, it was not a long-lasting transformative experience. This is not to say that a kundalini experience made in profound meditative or shamanic states cannot be transformative and accompanied with tremendous long-lasting insights, but I have come to believe the effects are more enduring and deeper when related to emotions, emotional energy, and the unblocking of them. In some ways, without the accompanying insight and connection to the source of emotions, the experience tends to stay encapsulated in a "bubble" of the altered state of consciousness.

The kundalini experience, as I have said, is not always pleasant and can even be dangerous. The physiologic response can be so intense as to cause a sympathetic nervous system overload and overstimulation with physical or mental consequences. Once, during a meditation group I was attending, a participant suddenly felt very faint with heart palpitations. I had her lie down and checked her out, asking the questions appropriate for determining the immediate medical course of action. She said she had just come out of a hot yoga session that had been very emotionally intense for her and that she had never had something like this happen before. I determined her symptoms did not indicate a serious medical problem and were not due to being overheated or dehydrated.

I worked on her energetically, beginning with getting her grounded. Attuning to her field, I sensed that she had begun to experience an emotional shock while meditating. Something had triggered her. Even though the group was not doing kundalini meditation, I suspected it had begun to rise during the hot yoga session. She got grounded, calmed down, and reverted to a stable state. Since we did not know each other well, it was not the appropriate place or time to talk about what had happened. Once she was stable, she thanked me, saying she had felt how the energy had shifted in her body. I invited her to contact me if she wanted, but I did not see her again.

Even if we experience the kundalini, we sometimes do so in a "bubble." When I lived in Los Angeles, I had a car accident. An eighteen-wheeler truck switched into my lane and crashed into my subcompact car. What I remember first was realizing that I was in trouble. To the left was a huge truck and to my right, a cliff past the guardrails. I cannot remember what happened. I went into a "bubble" that was bright and clear. When I came out of the bubble, I was uncomfortably close to the edge but safe and unhurt. Later, when I was working with Dr. Hunt, she interpreted this experience as a partial kundalini reflex: at the moment my life was in danger, I used the kundalini energy to connect with divine power and was able to keep myself safe. I needed a "bubble" because at that time in my own consciousness it was easier for me to deal with the great life-preserving energy surge in an altered state. It allowed me to use it without awareness, ownership, or responsibility for that power. The stronger the mind, the less need for the "bubble," and the more effective and powerful is the outcome.

I find that it is difficult for most of us to follow up on messages coming from our higher consciousness and to pursue our emotional blocks in order to evolve. There is a reason that we are reluctant to pursue these higher consciousness signals. The kundalini reflex is a life-preserving one, but because it arises in such extreme circumstances, it cannot always preserve the physical body and life. The kundalini experiences related to intense emotions that are part of past-life experiences are usually accompanied by fear. Fear occurs when the person realizes that the kundalini arising from emotions in another life resulted in death. Fear can also arise if the person experiences an occurrence when there was a desire to live or when the rising energy was so intense it needed to be stopped even at the risk of death. This information is stored in the field and is carefully and diligently suppressed because of the intensity of the original experience.

We need a continuous low-level flow of energy from the kundalini for health, creativity, and well-being. When the emotions associated with the experience are blocked, this constant flow is very weak or nonexistent and can contribute to illness, both physical and psychological. It is optimal, then, to not only know about the kundalini reflex but to have enough strength to use it most effectively when experienced. The rising of the kundalini becomes a transformative experience when it is related to complete awareness and resolution of the suppressed experience. In lifehood memory recovery, which I will describe in the following chapters, we do this by remembering and reliving the experience in the context of where it first occurred. In so doing, we release the intense emotions held in the mind and soul so that the kundalini energy can flow unhindered.

What I believe at this time about the kundalini is that all
three points of view are accurate. We can experience degrees of
kundalini energy flow, but we will not have a full awakening
until our consciousness is evolved enough and ready to accept the
responsibility and power that comes with it. It is a matter of our
soul's evolution.

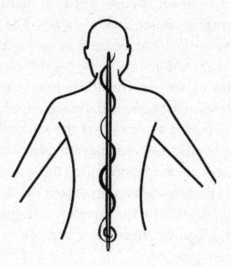

CHAPTER 16

REINCARNATION, PAST LIVES, AND LIFEHOODS

In the Introduction, I described my childhood experience of lying in my bed and rising to the edge of the universe. I described how at the time I interpreted this as my experience of smallness yet with the sensation that it was also my greatness. As startled as I was, the experience piqued my curiosity about what this vision meant and where understanding the meaning of the vision might lead me. My next question was about death and what happens when and after we die. I posed the question to my father, who is a scientist, a rational surgeon. He said we get buried, and that's the end. I was very uneasy with that answer, not just because of its finality and coldness, but because it simply *felt* wrong.

I had a friend who was Catholic. She convinced me we should be nuns. I obtained a set of plastic saints and learned about Catholicism, but the idea of heaven and hell bothered me. Did that mean everyone I loved—after all, we were Jewish—would be relegated to eternal damnation? That could not be right. What about the Hindus and Buddhists and Muslims? Too many people were excluded. Needless to say, my stint as a novice nun was short-lived.

I considered following the stricter tenets of my own religion. As comfortable and easy an alternative as it seemed to be to my unending questioning, the blind acceptance of orthodoxy and dogma of any sort was just unacceptable to me. At some point in my search, I learned of reincarnation. As farfetched as it seemed, something about the concept resonated with me. It followed with my belief, unformed and intuitive as it was, that the human mind, consciousness, and soul itself were too great and precious to simply live and die. Why would we be different from the rest of nature where the pattern of birth, death, and rebirth was constant? It made sense to me that life had a meaning that was deep and far reaching—that we were here to evolve, and just as all things evolve, so did the essence of who we are.

Throughout my life I had dreams that had a different quality from my usual dreams. In one dream I saw an older woman, in what I knew to be India, riding in a small boat on a river surrounded by beautiful trees. I knew in the dream the woman was me. The entire dream appeared as if it were a postcard received from a vaguely familiar place. I dismissed it as a dream. Later I saw that scenery in a movie and recognized it immediately.

As I got older and traveled extensively, I continued to have experiences that made me wonder if they were a sort of memory, although I had never been to that place before. Sometimes I could sense what might be energy or "see" something about the past in a place I had never visited before, but it was distinctly different from imagination, from visualizing how something might have been, or even what felt more like memory. Standing in a battleground of the Civil War, in spite of the silent, green pastures, all I wanted to do was escape the horror of what I felt and "saw" there. In Jerusalem at sunset, the golden overlay of light that filled the ancient city seemed both familiar and heart wrenching. In Machu Picchu, when I first arrived and before taking the tour that explained where I was, I stood in an empty field surrounded by ruins and became acutely aware of the vibrant life of a marketplace that had once pulsated there. I could see it; I could feel it. It was vivid and real.

Asian cultures had a familiarity to me. Some of my earliest childhood drawings were of women in kimonos. So much information about Tibet, India, Japan, and China felt inexplicably familiar, whether it was culture, art, philosophy, food, history, or tai chi sword. Many times I had internal images that seemed to be of these places as if they were memories, despite not traveling to Asia until decades later. In all these experiences, there was a reality and an emotional impact that was identifiably distinct from fantasy.

Not all new places had the same sense of familiarity. There were places I visited that were not accompanied by an intensely personal emotion. For the places that did have an impact, as real as they seemed, and after the "wow, that was really interesting" reaction, I did not pursue understanding the meaning of those emotions. I was either too young or too blocked to completely process what I was experiencing. But I was intrigued, and as I filed it all away, more questions began to formulate and take hold.

In my struggle to understand all this, I came to two conclusions: one was that there had to be an absolute truth about life, the essence of the human being, and about death, which was as yet unknown; the second was that this truth had to be true for all, without exception. If there was a heaven and hell, it had to be for everyone; if there was only the ground and dust, it had to be true for everyone; and if there was reincarnation, it had to be true for everyone. The idea that we have an evolving soul with a destiny and a purpose had to apply to us all, whether we were conscious of it or not. No theory, ideology, or belief that was exclusionary of any group of people could be true.

To speak of reincarnation is not easy. I am a person who questions and does not blindly accept a belief system. I have already written about my perennial tug-of-war between my scientist self and the intuitive/mystic self. As a physician I stayed in the intuitive closet for a long time. But more and more I found that when I spoke of my ideas, there were others who resonated with them. In fact, after my work with Psy-Ki and with Suzanne Lahl and Valerie Hunt, I no longer had any qualms about speaking openly. I found that the most surprising people, in the privacy of a one-on-one encounter, admitted to believing in reincarnation, energy fields or auras, that there was a greater meaning to their life, and to having a purpose or the soul destiny. These included businesspeople and executives of corporations, oilmen, Texas "red necks," CPAs, heiresses, judges, teachers, nurses, musicians, artists, nonprofessional people, and those who straddled all socioeconomic levels, countries, and cultures. Something seemed to resonate with more people than I would have suspected, regardless of their religion or upbringing, and that made me more curious and interested.

Evidence for Reincarnation

Although experiences related to reincarnation are predominantly anecdotally based, as a scientist I like to find evidence-based information to support hypotheses. To this end, I have been fascinated by the research on reincarnation done by Ian Stevenson, MD, and James Tucker, MD, at the University of Virginia. Theirs are the only large studies that seek to verify reported past-life memories by young children in various parts of the world. By getting details of the children's stories, they were able to confirm specific details of previous lives that these children claimed to have lived. Dr. Stevenson and Dr. Tucker have also done exhaustive research on the correlation between birthmarks and reports of past-life wounds or injuries. Dr. Tucker has published numerous papers and has developed methodology to measure the strength of claims made and to distinguish these claims from fantasy using statistical scales.[35] As difficult as it may seem to confirm that reincarnation is real, it is hard to refute the data that these researchers have amassed over many years. As yet, there is little we can say with absolute certainty about past lives or reincarnation, but I seek to enhance and elaborate on what we do know.

What is most convincing to me regarding the concept of past-life memories is the spontaneity with which imagery occurs and, more important, the emotional impact that often accompanies these experiences. In myself and in my patients, I have seen a profound depth of emotion that I rarely have experienced or seen in other therapeutic modalities. I have a fabulous imagination—I can fantasize, daydream, and tell stories with the best of them. But no matter how rich those imaginings may be, I have never felt the depth of emotion that I experienced in my work with Suzanne Lahl in what she called "mind dives," and with Valerie Hunt in what she called life-shock. I have witnessed this same depth of emotion in my own patients, even in people who have been with me for years and who have gone through the exploration of various methods of psychotherapy with me.

The people who have done the deeper lifehood sessions have reached clearer and more long-lasting resolutions than with any other treatment. This is not to say that the experience is true for all my patients. There are those who have not had dramatic transformations, some who have continued to need medications, and some who could go only partially into this kind of inner work. But the process is beneficial enough for me to write about what I have learned and what I believe to be true. I do so in the hope that you will find it to be a useful and meaningful way of understanding yourself as a human being—that this may be a way to perceive how you can live your life in the richest, most robust way, in your fullest capacities, and in the greatness of your soul.

What Is a Lifehood?

Reincarnation is defined as the rebirth of the soul into a new body after death. *Past life* is the term used to describe a specific experience of reincarnation. Valerie Hunt coined the term *lifehood*, which expands the definition of past life to describe the experience not as a snapshot of a past memory but in its totality from birth to death, including felt and repressed emotions. The totality of all experiences exists in the mind-field as packets of information, accessible through the mind and which influence patterns of behavior, the emotions, and the physical body of the current life.

The implications inherent in using the term lifehood are that there is something of the experience continuing to exist in our present. Just as we think of our *childhood* as memories that affect our present, so do our *lifehoods*. The details of the lifehood are in quanta information, or packets of information, existing as energy held within the mind-field for any individual soul. When there is reincarnation, these packets are reincarnated or carried along. Rather than referring to a snippet of memory to explain an isolated behavior as in the use of "past life," lifehood refers to a past-life set of memories within the context of the current personality, the soul, and the soul's destiny.

The most common way people come to learn of their own past lives is either through a psychic reading or a hypnotic regression. Psychic readers tap into the information in the bioenergy field through a very narrow lens. Hypnotic regression tends to focus on identifying a past life and finding one element that explains a particular symptom, behavior, or belief. Neither addresses the lifehood in its totality as a physical and soul experience, and neither addresses the importance of the continuity of the soul's destiny. Psychics do the work for the person, and hypnotherapists work while the person is in a semi-aware state. Neither is done in a way that allows the person to take full responsibility or have complete awareness, consciousness, and ownership of the experience.

Most often people use a past life as an explanation for their familiarity or comfort in a particular activity, skill, or profession.

They will say they did it in a previous life—for example, that they previously worked in healing professions. But then the question arises: If I am a healer because I have been one before, why do I have to be a healer again? If the purpose of reincarnation is evolution, doesn't it follow that once you evolve, you "get it," so why repeat it? Rather, the question should be this: If I have been a medicine man, a shaman, a priestess of the healing arts before, and I am a doctor again, what did I miss before, or what do I have to understand differently, that I am now repeating the experience?

We can answer the question by taking into account what we have already covered—how and where emotions are blocked at the deepest levels, leading to the perpetuation of patterns in choices, behavior, responses, and belief systems. The concept of lifehoods offers a template to resolve these higher consciousness emotional blocks by getting the information from the mind and the soul, thus releasing the blocked emotions and finally restructuring the field through a transformative change in the emotional energy. By going through this process, life can be inspired and the soul's destiny made manifest.

Lifehoods in Practice

In therapy and in the deeper knowing of ourselves, an important concept related to reincarnation is responsibility for the self. This issue becomes especially poignant when exploring our relationships with others. There are popular concepts related to reincarnation that have to do with the people in our lives. One is the idea that we choose a life with people we have known before, so we reincarnate to work things out with these same people or because we are comfortable with them. This may or may not be a true or even a useful point of view. Most significant is the recognition that what we are working out are the issues within ourselves.

I often pose this question to my patients: "Suppose you chose your parents and your family to be born into. Why do you think you would have made this choice?" Even with patients who do not believe in reincarnation, this question, posed hypothetically, can be a significant eye-opener. Many of us have become too comfortable and accepting in being the "victim." What this question does is to make us responsible for our choices; we can no longer blame others. We are put in a position to take full responsibility for the choices that we made in response to a situation, even in a situation where we appear to have no choice or truly had no choice. Of course, it would be inappropriate to pose this question to any person who has experienced extreme trauma in childhood if the person has not already resolved many of the issues related to this experience.

As much as I trust that these concepts are the ultimate source of knowing who we are, this level of work can be very difficult, and it is not appropriate in all situations. Just as we must go through preschool, kindergarten, elementary school, high school, and college, always building upon our fund of knowledge, so must we go through this building process to uncover the truth of who we are. Just as we would not expect an average kindergartener to successfully solve a calculus problem, we cannot expect everyone or every soul to be at the same level of evolution. In this regard, I am, and I encourage others to be, as nonjudgmental and compassionate as possible and respect a person's level of comprehension and acceptance, regardless of what it is. This does not mitigate the concept of reincarnation. Reincarnation reflects a choice that is made in the higher consciousness in order to evolve, and the essence of that evolution is to uncover, understand, and unblock emotions in order to resolve and break our pattern dynamics.

CHAPTER 17

LIFEHOOD MEMORY RECOVERY

We are now ready to tackle the more nitty-gritty aspects of resolving emotional blocks at the highest consciousness level. Much of what follows is, as yet, unfortunately anecdotal and empirical. Yet all hypotheses begin with the anecdotal and empirical before there is research to substantiate and verify. The instruments and research needed are not yet in existence (although Valerie Hunt came close to creating these instruments) to validate the complexities of the bioenergy field, the mind, and emotions. We may not have the science and technology to prove it all yet, but as I have stated, if there is truth to these ideas, eventually the truth will be revealed.

In the meantime, as a therapist and as one who has embarked wholeheartedly upon her own quest for growth, understanding, and evolution, I will use what appears to be effective until proven otherwise. I verbalize all this to preempt any defensiveness toward these ideas and to request, respectfully, that they be viewed with an open mind. To date, these concepts are the ones that have seemed to me the deepest, most profound, and the most enduring. What follows is a method of uncovering blocks at the deepest levels. These ideas evolved from working as a student and colleague with Valerie Hunt.

Creation of Emotional Blocks

Life-shock is a term coined by Valerie Hunt to describe the most intense traumatic experience leading to emotional blocks that can occur to a person, especially at the soul level. Such experiences, usually life threatening, are overwhelmingly beyond our ability to solve. In such life-threatening situations, the ingrained life-preserving reflex, or the kundalini response, is triggered. If you recall, it is described as a tremendous energy arising from the base of the spine and ascending to the top of the head, where it is released. This energy burst may be accompanied by body sensations and the internal experience of very bright light. Often there is great emotion followed by a sense of peace. This energy burst can manifest as great strength, agility, and clarity to deal with the threatening power facing us. It allows us to run faster, resist more strongly, and think more clearly.

When the kundalini rises, it is so intense that it is a shock to our consciousness. Over our lifetimes, or lifehoods, these shocks add up and determine the choices we make. They affect our beliefs, fears, and patterns of behavior. Because these shocks are so intense, they carry with them tremendous emotional energy and are blocked from our ordinary memory and then stored in altered states of consciousness. This energy, with its accompanying information, is recorded in the brain and held in the body, where it is manifested in physiological disturbances and emotional stresses. If the shock was processed effectively, life-preserving energy, or the kundalini energy, is always flowing in small amounts to give us vitality, power, creativity, and health. Most often, however, this life-force energy is blocked and therefore not processed or experienced. This can lead to a pattern of weak energy, low vitality, lack of creativity, and a sense of powerlessness.

The Four R's

Problems of the soul occur at the time of an intense, tragic, or catastrophic experience that caused an impulsive, emotional judgment with behaviors to defend or protect the soul. Because of the intensity of emotion, complete forgetfulness follows. Having cognitive knowledge of the patterns associated with these problems or having willpower alone does not automatically lead to change or resolution of the problems. What may lead to awareness and insight are what I describe as the four R's:

1. *Recovering* the memory

2. *Reliving* the experience

3. *Rescripting*, which creates a new perception of the root emotional causes of the problems

4. *Resolution*, which leads to clarity about oneself, freeing a person to be creative, energized, effective, and more self-aware

With that, life can become an inspired one, and the soul is able to fulfill its destiny.

Valerie Hunt developed life-shock sessions, a technique for identifying and resolving trauma of the human soul. Suzanne Lahl referred to these sessions as *mind dives*, and I have come to call the process lifehood memory recovery. The four R's occur in the course of a lifehood memory recovery session. In conducting these sessions, Valerie Hunt, Suzanne Lahl, and I, in our respective practices, were able to identify correlations between the insights made from sessions with a significant degree of resolution and dynamic, profound transformations. These transformations occurred in a person's belief systems, behavior, capacity to function, and even health. The process is not entirely different from other forms of insight-oriented psychotherapy.

As a psychiatrist who has specialized in PTSD with veterans of war, child-abuse patients, and rape victims, I will be the first to admit that the general process for coming to terms with and resolving these experiences is basically the same. What makes this process unique is its emphasis on the totality of an experience—one that may not have occurred in this life and yet carries with it a deep emotional impact.

Lifehood memory recovery focuses predominantly on lifehoods and deeply ingrained soul trauma with the attendant pattern dynamics. Not all people who come to work with me are comfortable with the idea of reincarnation (including, at times, the skeptical scientist within me). With them I take the attitude that the images that arise may be used as metaphor; the emergence of imagery can be made more comfortable and acceptable when seen as symbolic of the issues with which they deal. Surprisingly, people do not experience the imagery as symbolic or metaphorical as often as you might think. It is common for people to spontaneously identify the imagery as being of themselves in another life.

Even in my personal experience of mind dives and life-shock sessions, I have been left stunned and needing to absorb an experience because of its impact. Seeing these scenarios taking place in different times and in different places seemed to explain some of the mystery about my ways of thinking, my interests, choices I have made, and my perceptions of myself and my place in this world. I have never questioned the truth and the reality of the experiences. Just as I would not question a vivid memory from my childhood with its details, senses, and emotions, I find it difficult to question these lifehood memories. There is something inherently different in the quality of these images from the imagery that arises from imaginings, daydreams, and fantasy. I will be curious to see, as this exploration evolves into research, how these differences will be quantified.

There are those who challenge the idea that all memory is accurate in this life, much less a past one, and I will concede to this argument. However, I believe enough is accurate for us to be able to understand that what is being perceived is meaningful and significant—and, as I have said, the telling point itself is found in the accompanying emotions. Many of my patients recognize on their own that there is something "flat" about the experience when they veer off into descriptions that do not ring as true.

None of this is to say that our past lives explain everything about who we are and why we are the way we are. There is a complex interplay between the information held in our soul, mind, bioenergy field, and physical body. Although we may determine that all manifestations within the physical body, including disease, originate in the bioenergy field, for now this does not mean that we can completely change what might already be genetically, biologically, or even physiologically present. We are, after all, divine *human beings*, and as such, we must recognize and embrace not only the potential power of our divine nature but also our vulnerability and the fragility of our human nature.

Lifehood Memory Recovery Session

What occurs during a lifehood memory recovery session is a methodical uncovering of information that has been locked away in the mind and bioenergy field—the information packets in the field. First an evaluation is conducted to focus on what the perceived patterns are: where you feel stuck or held back in your life, what you desire and want for yourself, what your goals are, and what keeps you from their fulfillment. Unfulfilled social, financial, medical, religious, and professional needs or problems are identified. This is mere information gathering, and at this point, there is no attempt to find out the whys. Often we use kinesiology to get answers.

I go into more detail about kinesiology in the appendix. What I did not emphasize earlier is that kinesiology can be done verbally or nonverbally. You might wonder how a communication might be nonverbal. If we start with the premise that everything generates energy, then you can see how even our thoughts can generate energy. This may be the basis of telepathy. I have seen nonverbal communication demonstrated many times.

One of the more dramatic examples occurred in my office with a patient who suffered severe anxiety brought on by the belief that a *bruja*, or witch, had cursed her. Most of the time she was very responsive to her therapy sessions and treatment, but on this particular day she was inconsolable, unable to talk, and in a complete state of panic. Not knowing what else to do, I asked her to sway just when she felt like it. (I describe how to do the sway in the appendix.) Using the techniques from Psy-Ki, I asked questions silently. She swayed only at the end of every question. As she did so, she slowly calmed down. We cleared the blocks using the meditation I describe in the appendix, and she not only calmed but showed great clarity in her communication. What calmed her? Was it telepathic interaction? Was it coincidental motions of swaying? Was it shifting the energy in her field from disruptive (anticoherent) to calm (coherent)? I do not have the answer. I simply accepted what I witnessed and took a leap of faith, trusting the experience.

In a memory recovery session, I usually ask a question nonverbally first, note the answer, then repeat it verbally, and note the answer. Asking nonverbally first helps to eliminate censoring or blocking of information and is often the best validation of answers given. What we seek is a general framework of information that will be brought into clearer focus in the course of the session. The questions focus on locations, time periods, and cultures that may be significant.

Then you lie down on a massage table in order to be comfortable and eliminate distractions. This is optional; the session can proceed just as well with you sitting comfortably. Your field is read to identify energy blocks and then prepared by spinning the chakras to open your mind and field and stabilize it. This usually facilitates the flow of information. Then we go through the four R's. I repeat here the four R's of a lifehood memory recovery session.

- *Recovering*—the process of getting detailed information
- *Reliving*—the process of remembering and allowing the emergence of emotions
- *Rescripting*—the process of finding a new perspective
- *Resolving*—the process of integrating and coming to terms with an experience

Recovering

The initial stage is recovering, which means remembering by allowing memories to come into awareness. In the initial evaluation, I usually ask questions that will give clues about the source of the relevant memories and the origin of soul trauma. These may include questions about countries, cultures, and time periods that are significant. I often use kinesiology while asking the relevant questions to obtain more specific information. As the process gets underway with guided imagery, a person will have spontaneous memories and images arise that give increasing amounts of detail. To facilitate this process, I often use the image of the blank screen in a movie theater. I ask the person to see themselves as an audience member waiting to see what comes up on the screen. Often what is seen has been surprising to both the person experiencing it and to me.

In following the evolving scenario, more and more information is described. Most often what a person visualizes is related to past-life experiences, but sometimes what needs to be resolved first may be a pre-birth issue or a this-life issue. You may be questioning how you can have a memory in the womb, but remember that we are looking at the information packets that you carry with you in the bioenergy field, which are present even before birth. You may be responding to information in your mother's field. The pattern dynamics brought in may have an impact even at that point. In all situations, I maintain complete respect for the wisdom of the soul and psyche. Whatever experiences are more dominant and pressing, whether past life, pre-birth, or current life, are the ones we pursue.

In other words, the process of coming to terms with trauma is not a neat and tidy one. There is jumping back and forth and digressions and detours, or what a patient of mine called "stepping stones." These are sometimes necessary because they are less traumatic, more dominant in the consciousness, or safer to look at first. The recovering process can therefore be somewhat messy, occurring in bursts and spurts and not sequentially or chronologically.

If you think about how you recall a memory, you realize that it rarely comes sequentially or chronologically. You will most likely remember one element: "Oh, yeah, it was my tenth birthday, and I had a great cake and I remember waking up excited and I got so many presents, and when I first woke up, everyone came in and sang happy birthday . . ." You get the picture—not sequential but coming into more detail and greater clarity little by little.

The first images that usually come in are about the physical characteristics of the person whose life is being perceived. These may come in slowly and, like a movie shot, come into clearer and clearer focus as if from a distance. To determine the age of the person, I will ask, "What do her hands look like?" To determine the place, I will ask for a description of the environment; to identify the time period or gender, I will ask for details about clothes, physical appearance, and style of structures. If it were a movie shot, it would come into focus and then pan out to get the overall picture. It is important to obtain as many details as possible about appearance, clothing, and even feeling states by asking about them.

After I gather the specifics of the surroundings, the environment, and the first person seen (who is almost always identified as the self in another life), then I will ask if there are other people present. From there, more and more details come into perception. In this way there is increasing clarity until a complete story emerges. During this process, it is important to ask questions carefully without influencing the answers—that is, no leading questions such as "Are you wearing a toga?" Instead ask, "What are you wearing?"

Reliving

Once the details about a life begin to emerge, the person is encouraged to experience it as vividly as possible. This usually happens spontaneously, and there is little need to coach. As the therapist-guide, I continue to ask broad questions that will bring the images and sensations into clearer focus, and eventually a complete description of a life or event unfolds. In the case of a lifehood experience, details of the life from birth to death are clarified. This is reliving the life. Often this process is arduous, does not come easily, and can even take several sessions.

The person eventually will make a close identification with the consciousness of the person whose life is being viewed. He or she will then move throughout the events of that life to the moment of the intense, tragic, or catastrophic event. There is a focus on details from both an external point of view and an internal emotional point of view. We pay attention to the limitations, insecurities, and strengths that determined the decisions and behavior at the time. This allows the past personality's behaviors, decisions, and source to be revealed with clarity.

Often the current personality will experience intense emotions and a desire to avoid them as information becomes clearer. Coming to terms with an experience, unblocking emotions, and reaching a point of resolution may take several sessions, each time revisiting one lifehood and each time unfolding deeper layers of understanding. There may be times that the person identifies so strongly with the past personality that they lose sight of who they are now. For this reason it is important to facilitate the process with compassion, guidance, and constant mindfulness. I always encourage the person to feel their emotions fully and to allow whatever emotions they are experiencing to flow, openly and freely. I remind them that the experience was from a past version of themselves and to stay aware of who they are now.

These emotions are not to be confused with catharsis, which is a release of emotions, but is more of what might be called *anagnorisis*. I love the idea of what this word represents. Anagnorisis derives from Greek and means "to make known." It refers to a moment in a plot or story where the main character either recognizes or identifies his/her true nature, recognizes another character's true identity, or discovers the true nature of his situation, or that of the others—leading to the resolution of the story.

We see anagnorisis in movies and books all the time. It is the plot twist. An example would be the moment that Darth Vader says to Luke Skywalker, "I am your father." We see the impact of that truth on the main character's face and we see the responsibility and the implications of that revelation.

The recognition of the truth when confronting the scenes of the past life, when the person recognizes the implications of decisions made for which only they were responsible that resulted in situations causing emotional blocks, may release profound emotions. This is the anagnorisis. The emotions arise from not only unleashing the blocks, but from the awareness that there is responsibility for blocking them initially—in other words, the truth of the situation. When someone relives a lifehood, that person's consciousness is expanded to include current and past personalities, allowing for the beginning of an integration of experiences. This leads to greater awareness about where a behavior occurred or a decision was made, the source of the blocked emotions, and how the consequences have repeated in the form of pattern dynamics.

Rescripting

Rescripting is just as its name suggests: an opportunity to look at an experience and essentially "rewrite" or envision a new response. Although this may sound like a futile endeavor (after all, you might say, you can't change the past), it is actually an invaluable tool for seeing a different perspective. More than changing perspective alone, rescripting allows us to physically change the structure of the bioenergy field. The reason for this will become clear when you recall that it is emotions that structure the field. There is a pivotal point where intense emotions become blocked, leading to complete forgetfulness about the decision and behavior. This point is the true source of the emotional block, and it is here where change can occur.

Rescripting is a profound process through which the intense experience is again relived, this time with all the emotions that arose at the time and guided by the higher self. In this way, the exact experience is relived with a greater appreciation for what could have been done differently. Together, the current personality and the past personality can have deeper insight. With this deeper insight, there is an unblocking, with the emotional freedom to choose a better, wiser, and more appropriate behavior or decision, leading to a different energetic response. As you already learned, different energy patterns in the field restructure the field itself so that the emotional discharge and reworking of the trauma result in a restructuring of the bioenergy field/mind-field. This leads to changing the pattern dynamics. It is like finding a new path to take and getting out of the proverbial rut.

Identifying and reliving the trauma or shock experience and all the other things that came with it, feeling the true and uncensored emotions, releasing the emotional barriers, and then rescripting, allows a person to feel the availability of a new power. There is recognition and admission that the belief systems and patterns of behavior arose from problems of the past-life personality. It becomes easier to see that the problems came from that life and that the level of awareness and beliefs from that life are no longer effective or don't work in this life. By putting experiences of the lifehood in the context of the current personality, it is then possible to do the rescripting and even restructuring of the field.

Rescripting can be partial or complete. In a partial rescripting, there may be new insights and transformation, but the true source of the soul trauma and opening of the energy block may not have been fully reached. This does not mean that change and transformation cannot occur. Every new insight and shift in perspective can be a valuable progression toward deeper and more profound insights and perspectives. Often it is necessary to experience less intense events with incomplete understanding in order to lay the groundwork for the more intense and profound ones. Complete rescripting occurs when the energy tied to the earlier life-threatening charge of the kundalini experience is combined with conscious awareness of current feelings, emotions, and thoughts and is then released and allowed to flow.

Resolving

During the session and following it, the person is encouraged to be with or think about the experience of the lifehood personality; often he or she will notice shifts in appearance or demeanor of that personality. The person may notice that both he or she and the lifehood personality speak differently or take different actions. This awareness of the current personality and the lifehood personality allows for integration within the consciousness. The person then can develop a new profound plan of action and insight with expansion of coherent patterns. He or she is more readily able to identify the past pattern dynamics that were faulty, seemingly unchangeable, and enslaving over the span of lifehoods, and then replace them. The person is likely to experience deep emotions with a sense of relief (catharsis), openness, excitement, and vitalized energy. Finally, he or she will experience a sense of connection to the spiritual—the divine—and to the potential and power in his or her life and soul's evolution. Using his or her unique life skills, the person can achieve creative rescripting and resolution.

When the mind-field energy has been restructured and rescripting is complete, the person feels settled, calm, and whole. There is a sense of strength, transformation, and lightness that is physical, emotional, and spiritual, and the greatness of his or her soul can now shine. We may choose to repeat this entire process at another time with other lifehoods, allowing the person to develop greater and greater awareness of himself or herself.

Many times I have seen my patients return after such a session having made significant changes in their lives and beliefs about themselves and their place in the world. Examples include the following:

- a woman was finally able to end a destructive relationship

- a cancer patient was able to connect with her internalized anger and live the rest of her life with acceptance, joy, and openness

- an anxious and depressed person had a transformation after the recognition and realization of why she repressed and did not tolerate her tremendous intuitive capacity

- entrepreneurs, artists, writers, and musicians who were stuck and blocked or could not see that they were self-sabotaging their success were able to unleash their creativity and productivity

The transformation of lives, the enhancements of relationships, the degree of self-awareness and self-acceptance, and the embracing of personal empowerment that have occurred have amazed me. Such stories have tempered my doubts and kept me passionate about the privilege of working with those courageous enough to undergo this level of personal work.

CHAPTER 18

LIFE'S DESTINY AND THE INSPIRED LIFE

What do *life destiny* and *soul destiny* mean? Is it different for each of us, or is there something universal that we are all meant to achieve? Our destiny can be seen as our template or plan that we are following in order to expand our consciousness and enhance our awareness. In some ways our destinies are personal, determined by the sum total of who we are and who we have been. Yet as human beings, we all have the same ultimate destiny—to reach our highest capacity, to live life fully, to communicate and manifest this capacity, and to grow and evolve. It is the same for all of us—it is universal. How it is manifested will be unique to you. It does not matter whether you achieve your destiny as an artist, a gardener, a doctor, a teacher—soul destiny is not about the specific job. What matters is a complete manifestation of your capacity that brings a sense of grounding, wholeness, and soul gratification.

Your interests, your passions, your intellect, and your level of consciousness will determine the specific work you choose. Even though the word *destiny* implies a predetermined fate, we always have choices. The important thing is to live as close to your truth as possible, to know yourself fully, and to be authentic in the choices you make. This type of life requires courage: courage to examine yourself, to challenge the beliefs that limit you, and to go against your culture, society, or even family if you cannot manifest your truth otherwise. It requires embracing and accepting all the vulnerabilities that come with being human, such as sickness, pain, fragility, or making mistakes. It requires taking full responsibility of being divine, not in a religious sense, but in a spiritual one—by owning and taking responsibility for your power; by becoming creative, wise, compassionate; and by knowing you are a part of a universal consciousness. This is what it means to be a divine human. It is risky to face yourself, to unblock where you are stuck, to make changes, and to transform. Yet it is liberating to live in your truth, to be honest about who you are and want to be, to express your creativity, and to experience life in the richest way possible.

You will find that it is exhilarating to live an inspired life. To be able to do so, you must keep in mind what you have learned. We repeat observable patterns (pattern dynamics) that result from transactions based on the structure of the field, determined by emotions blocked by trauma and shock in this life and/or past lifehoods. These blocked emotions and patterns hold the soul back from fulfilling its destiny, which is to be a divine human and to manifest that in the world. The mind-field is where true transformation occurs. For that to happen, you must do the following:

- Trust the guidance from your intuition.
- Find the source of your blocked emotions.
- Acknowledge, experience, express, and own the truth of those emotions.
- Restructure the bioenergy field.
- Engage in transactions.
- Elaborate your life.

Realize that this is a long, arduous, experiential, and exciting process that will continue throughout your life. But the journey is worth it. It results in living a full-spectrum life, having physical strength and the ability to protect your life, solving problems, and being confidently creative, intuitive, intelligent, spiritually inspired, and divinely empowered. Then you can manifest your highest capacity in this world, reaching the destiny your soul has created, and being the divine human you are meant to be.

It begins with expanded self-awareness
guiding you to live an inspired life.

You may get there in this life or the next,
but you must persist in the journey.

Every aspect of your being is demanding it.

EXERCISES FOR YOUR MIND-FIELD AND EMOTIONS

The Most Important Questions to Ask Yourself

As you go through the exercises/meditations, hold the following important questions as your foundation and intention. How you answer is the biggest clue to finding out who you are and what your life's purpose is.

1. Who am I at this time?
2. What defines me?
3. What am I feeling at this time?
4. What do I desire most? (To understand this question, go

beyond the basic, material desires. Think about the meaning of your life and why you are in this life)

5. What is keeping me from having what I desire most?

6. What am I saying no to?

7. What is my deepest truth that I ignore?

Emotional Energy

These questions and exercises will help you identify the emotions that affect you most deeply. They will help you recognize how you transact with others, giving you information about your own blocked emotional energy.

Anger

1. What makes me angry? What makes me the angriest?

2. Where and how in my body do I experience anger?

3. Where do I put my energy when I am angry?

4. What makes me feel frustrated and what do I do about it?

5. What do others do that makes me angry?

6. What makes me angry in relationships?

7. What makes me angry in business or work?

8. What makes me angry in my culture?

9. Is there something specific that triggers anger within me, something that I know or sense has been distorted?

10. When and how old was I the first time I got really angry? What experience comes to mind, and what are the emotions connected to the experience?

11. Are there certain people who always make me angry? Try to find traits or characteristics that these people share.

Pay attention to what comes up in your mind, focusing only on the emotional experience.

Fear

1. What makes me most fearful?

2. Where and how in my body do I experience fear?

3. What specifically triggers fear within me that I know or sense has been distorted?

4. What makes me afraid in my culture?

5. What makes me afraid in relationships?

6. What makes me afraid in business or work?

7. Who are the people I may be afraid of or that I avoid? Try to find traits or characteristics that these people share.

8. When and how old was I when I felt the most frightened? What experience comes to mind, and what are the emotions connected to the experience?

Pay attention to what comes up in your mind, focusing only on the emotional experience.

Love

1. What aspects of love are easy for me?

2. What specific experiences of love were easy for me?

3. What aspects of love are difficult for me?

4. What specific experiences of love were difficult for me?

5. When in my life did I feel most loved? What was that experience like?

6. Do I ignore warning signals or red flags when I fall in love with someone? What are the similarities in these situations?

7. Am I aware of emotionally unfinished business that I carry around? Describe it.

8. What are the qualities in the people I love?

Questions to Stimulate Your Mind Capacity

Creativity and Skills

1. In what ways am I creative?

2. How am I expressing my creativity?

3. What gives me pleasure?

4. What are my skills?

5. What are my capacities?

6. In what ways do I manifest or act on my capacities?

7. How do I hold myself back or "slam on the brakes"?

Emotions

1. How would I describe myself at this time in my life?

2. What emotions are easy for me?

3. What emotions do I have difficulty experiencing or expressing?

4. What emotions do I avoid feeling?

5. How do I deal with emotions when they come up? When they are intense?

6. What have been the most shocking events of my life?

7. How have I handled my biggest emotional challenges?

Mystical and Spiritual

1. Do I have strong attractions to or feel inexplicably drawn to other countries, cultures, or historical periods? Where and what are they?

2. What experiences have I had that I could not explain?

3. Have I had experiences that felt transcendent or made me feel as if I were at one with all things? How did I handle those experiences?

4. Where do I find spirituality?

5. What is my connection to my soul, highest consciousness, and/or the divine? How do I communicate or listen to that part of myself?

6. What is my purpose in this life?

7. What is my destiny?

Exercise to Access Mind/Cell Memory

Focus your mind on experiencing the cellular aggravation and the emotional frustration active in you right now. Pay attention to what crosses your mind even if it seems unrelated to now.

Ask yourself if you have ever before had the same symptoms, pain, or conditions that you are currently experiencing. Do not do an intellectual time survey, listing each time, but rather try to get a generalized sense of those experiences. Particularly focus on the ones where the same situations, places, or feelings existed. Now you are accessing your mind/cell memory.

Let this memory become as elaborate as it was in the past. Ask if there were other similar experiences that have fortified the cell memory. Sometimes the memory is highly specific as to areas of the body, for example, the digestive or nervous systems, the heart, or muscles. Many times it is general, like inflammation or functionality; it worsens at night or at certain times of the year.

Do not try to use a logical, linear approach with a formula—it won't work.

Over time, accumulate information on a conscious level until the picture is clear. When the associated emotions are patterned and you are willing to experience all the memories, you will be able to find a resolution.

You will be amazed at what can happen if you give up the idea that "this is me," who you are, biologically or genetically. Accept that what you experienced is not your identity. The mind/cell has both the information and the answers correctly, beyond what you think you know. That knowledge may be key in your healing, even if you continue to use traditional medical interventions.

Preparation for Opening the Mind-Field[36]

There are three parts in the preparation for opening the mind and accessing the mind-field information. Do this when you can be alone without interruptions or distraction, preferably lying down, but any comfortable position is fine. As you become more proficient, you will find that this process occurs more easily and quickly.

Quieting

Quieting means to relax the body and the mind. As you go through the exercise, focus on each part of the body and take your time to feel tightness by actually tightening that area as much as you can and really feel the contrast and difference when you release it. To facilitate quieting, in order to maximize the muscle relaxation, it may help to imagine yourself as a rag doll.

1. Begin by releasing any tension you are initially aware of. Take a few deep breaths in, and then let them out. Repeat this until you feel yourself calming, releasing, and relaxing. (The best way to breathe is diaphragmatically by imagining you are inflating and then deflating a balloon in your belly. If your shoulders are moving up and down, you are not breathing diaphragmatically!)

2. Focus on your feet and legs: tighten and then release the tension in them. Feel them getting heavy.

3. Focus on your hips and butt: tighten and then release the tension in them. Feel them drop heavily downward; let them go soft and limp.

4. Focus on your arms and shoulders: tighten and then release the tension in them. Feel them sinking into the floor.

5. Focus on your head and neck: tighten and then release the tension in them. Imagine that your neck is sagging and loose.

6. Be aware of your feelings.

Grounding

1. Now that you have released all the tension from your body, make sure you are grounded. To do this take a deep breath from the bottom of your feet.

2. Feel the energy coming up your legs up to your belly.

3. Exhale that same energy up to your chest and out of the crown at the top of your head.

4. Repeat until you can feel the energy moving up from your feet and out the crown and it begins to feel like an established circuit.

Expanding

1. Feel the energy that you have been moving smoothly getting bigger and bigger and expanding outward.

2. Expand the energy of your feet and legs outward.

3. Expand the energy of your belly and chest outward.

4. Expand the energy of your neck and head outward.

5. Expand the energy of your arms outward.

6. Notice your boundaries getting bigger and your energy field reaching further and further. Be alert to sensations, and increase your awareness of sensory input.

7. Rest and be aware of your overall field. Now that it is expanded, be aware of the thoughts, images, and sensations that have been coming in. Do not censor or judge. Describe to yourself what you are experiencing, and then record your experience and reactions in your journal.

The purpose of this exercise is to get to know yourself in order to receive the information the mind has and to come to understand it. The ultimate goal is to open the closed areas of your mind, access your hidden agendas, identify your restricting thoughts, and begin to reorder your emotions, especially if they are confused. This may take time and repetition. The imagery and information that comes in may or may not be the most accurate, but remember that all information is data. Even if the data are inaccurate, you will learn to feel the difference between accurate and inaccurate information when you are aware of your responses.

As you go through the process, think of yourself as the greatest explorer of yourself. You want to gather as much data as you can to become aware of your transactions with inside and outside stimuli. Eventually the imagery and information will be clearer to you and their meanings revealed.

Meditations for Accessing Mind-Field Information

The following visualizations/meditations will help you get meaningful information held in your mind-field about your deepest self. This information is about you, your belief systems, and your past experiences that affect you now. Be patient with yourself as you go through this session. Honor what you may and may not be able to do in one session. It is fine to repeat the process several times, allowing yourself to go deeper each time. Think of it as a dive, as in scuba diving. You have to go slowly to acclimate yourself, and as you get more comfortable, the depths you can go to become greater. Stay with the process as long as you can, pushing yourself as much as possible, even if the emerging information makes you uncomfortable or uneasy. Always begin each session with the exercise for opening the mind-field. Do not try to do too much all at once. If at any point you feel unsafe or overwhelmed, or unable to tolerate what is coming in, stop and wait until you can work with someone who can guide you.

(You may want to read the visualization out loud while recording yourself so that you can follow it comfortably later).

Being with the Mind/Soul

Let's take an imagined trip where your mind/soul will show you the way. Start walking, and notice the surface you are walking on. Notice the terrain and sky. See the objects in the environment. If your mind changes your path, follow along and observe the new details. Don't try to control the process; just relax and trust in it. You may see water. Notice what it is like. Is it warm or cool? Look to see if anything is in it or if images are reflected from it. Notice if there are any structures. If some do appear, go in and look around. If you meet people, note what they are wearing, what they look like, how they seem. Interact with them if you wish. Remember you are merely observing. You are not analyzing, judging, or trying to make logical sense out of anything that you see, sense, or experience.

Continue walking. Find your house of consciousness. As you learned before, it can be anything that you want it to be. It can be based on reality or fantasy and even defy the laws of gravity. Make it as detailed as you wish, both outside and inside. Take your time, and enjoy making this place exactly what you want it to be. It may even be different from the house you built at another time. Walk in and notice the details of the interior. Notice what it feels like to you. Make it as welcoming, as cozy, and as uniquely yours as you wish. When you are all settled in, find a comfortable place to be still.

Invite your mind/soul, your highest consciousness, to join you. Just note what form it takes, how it appears to you. What is its character? How does it feel to you? Notice how you feel being with it. Tell your mind/soul that you desire to be open to all the information that is there—that you are ready to know your truth. Wait and listen to whatever your mind/soul tells, shows, or gives you at this time. Take your time, as much time as you need.

When you are ready, thank your mind/soul for the information and its presence. Tell it that you will listen and pay attention to it more often and that you are eager to accept its guidance so that you may have expanded self-awareness and consciousness. Take a moment simply to be there with it, knowing that this is you. When you are ready, walk out of your house to return on the path you came from to your starting place. Know that where you have been is a place where you can be with your highest self at any time, whenever you want.

This-Life Information[37]

Begin by repeating the exercise for opening the mind. To enhance your ability to stay grounded while at the same time maintaining the flexibility to receive information, you may imagine that you have a soft, flexible cord tied around your waist with the other end tied to something strong and solid, like a boulder. This is a very long cord that you can extend as you fly upward or you can retract to bring your feet back to the ground. Take time to practice flying up and looking around and then slowly bringing yourself down. When you are on the ground, you feel grounded.

Suppose you chose your parents, your family, and the circumstances of your life. Ask yourself why you chose your parents for this lifehood. Don't think in terms of blaming them, but rather focus upon them as genetic, biological parents or as people who created a particular environment for you to be raised in. They are people who endowed you with certain qualities and created challenges for you.

Suppose you chose the country and century of your birth. Ask yourself why you have chosen that country and this time. See yourself as a fetus inside your mother's body. At approximately what point did your soul enter the fetus to become you? Were you and your mother ready and cooperative at your birth? Remember your birth experience. Was it a simple or a difficult birth? Do you know about your mother's experience at your birth? Even if you do not know or cannot find out, sense her consciousness about you and her experience. As any information comes in, pay attention to it and the emotions that arise with it. If they are difficult or painful, try to shift your perception to see if you can have a new understanding or insight.

What were your first memories of this earth? Spontaneously, without thinking about it, choose an age. See yourself at that age. Look at the surroundings. Where are you? What are you wearing? If you are with other people, observe what they are doing. What thoughts cross your mind? When these images fade, choose another age to see yourself. Eventually ask what age you least remember. That age may be the most important. Get as much information as you can, keeping in mind that you can return to this later. When you feel you have enough information for now, slowly bring yourself to the present, to your room and your body.

Take time to write down your experience.

Lifehood Information

You are going to go on a journey to gather information about a specific lifehood. As you begin on your path, you will receive instructions along the way. If a sign shows up, read it. If you see a package, open it. If someone approaches you, hear what the person has to say. This is the mind's way of giving you a peek before disclosing bigger things.

As you continue walking, notice your environment. What is the terrain like? Is it mountainous, jungle, or desert-like? Notice if there are dwellings and what they look like. Ask where you are. If your answer is too vague or general, ask for the specific country or continent. Things may change along the way. If they do, it is fine—just notice the changes, and wait for the information to come into clarity.

Look around for the presence of other people. Notice how they are dressed and what they are doing. Notice how you are dressed. Look down at your feet to see what you have on them. Look at your hands to see if they are large or small, what color they are, and whether they look masculine or feminine. Look at your clothes. Are you male or female? What age are you? Look at where you live. What kind of structure is it? What is your family like—your mother, your father? Do you have brothers and sisters? Get as much detail as you can.

If you question this experience, feeling that you are just making it all up, remember that sometimes real clues occur through metaphor or what you think is imagination. You might find it strange that you can "see" yourself outside yourself. You may fluctuate from this perspective to one that is not observing from the outside but from the inside. This is normal since you are at the same time both the one experiencing the past and the observer of it as yourself in the present.

Spontaneously recall events from that time. See yourself as a very young child, then an older one, a teenager, a young adult. Just notice what this person is like: what thoughts the person has, what skills and abilities, how he or she makes decisions and choices, what cultural beliefs exist, what this person feels, shows, or keeps hidden. Notice any emotions that come up. If you find an age that carries a large emotional impact with it, ask yourself if this is something you have experienced in your current life. Let the story unfold.

See yourself in old age. Follow that life to its termination at whatever age that transpired. Reflect on the life. Was it a passive or an active one? What were your beliefs, your consciousness? Do you feel you accomplished what you came into that life to do? Where did you get stuck? How did you die? Did you want to die to remove yourself from an impossible situation or did you fight to the end? What were your emotions in that life? Take note of anything that arises. If you feel emotions welling, do not try to stop them. Allow them to flow freely.

Reflect with the personality of that life and with your current consciousness about that life, the choices, decisions, and emotional patterns that you experienced. How might things have been handled differently? What other choices and decisions could you have made? If it was all done passively, ask yourself if that person with that consciousness would have felt differently, if he or she had fought for life, even if the outcome was the same. Experience all the possibilities together. Allow any new insight or knowledge to come in.

When no more information is coming in or you recognize a new insight or understanding, be with that person who was you, thank him or her, and prepare to return. Slowly come back and write your experience.

Mind and Emotions Self-Assessment

After each exercise, describe the experience to yourself as if you were talking to a friend, and then ask yourself the following:

- What questions were answered?
- What questions do I still have?
- What did I experience physically?
- What did I experience emotionally?
- What was the hardest part of the exercises/visualizations/meditations?
- What new perspectives and/or insights have I gained?
- What is the potential for my growth from this experience?

Open-Heart Meditation[38]

The final visualization I would like to offer you is one that can be done at any time when you feel unsettled, in need of centering, or when you need to shift your perspective. We will be selectively visualizing the color pink. This is deliberate. Pink is associated with tenderness, compassion, universal and unconditional love. Again, you may want to read the visualization out loud while recording it so that you can follow it comfortably later.

1. Begin by opening your energy field, which helps to open your mind-field where intuitive information comes in.
2. Close your eyes; take a deep breath.
3. Breathe through the bottom of your feet, in through your left and out through the right.
4. Breathe through your knees, through your elbows, through your shoulders.

5. Next you will breathe into the major energy centers using specific colors. Begin at the space between your legs and breathe the color red.

6. Breathe in through the area around your pubic bone in the color orange.

7. Breathe in through your belly in the color yellow.

8. Breathe in through your heart in the color green; feel the warmth and openness there.

9. Breathe in through your throat in the color blue.

10. Go to the top of your head and breathe in a crystal clear white.

11. Connect fully with your body. Release every tension in your body.

With your next breath, visualize breathing the color pink. Fill your body with this color, let it blanket you outside and glow within you—every cell, every atom, every molecule, and all the spaces in between. Let it fill you and open your heart. With each breath, know that there are vibrant beats of your heart. Allow this pink light to surround your heart, to glow within, opening it even more.

As you fill your body with this soft pink light, as it courses through you, feel yourself expanding until the pink light merges with you. And as you exhale, visualize this light spilling out through your breath and your heart extending to the person next to you. If you are alone, begin by extending this pink breath to anyone who is close to you or who is near you.

Expand this light to reach the person next to him or her, and keep expanding until your room is so filled with this light that it spills outside the room extending further to envelope the street, the neighborhood, the trees, the sky, reaching all the people you love and then others who are important in your life. Keep expanding this warm and vibrant pink luminescence, which has reached all in your intimate circle, expanding to your acquaintances, your coworkers, everyone you know.

This light is so abundant you can even embrace those people who might be challenging to you or even those you think you do not like. Remember you are simply including them in this pink light, not engaging with them. See how you have expanded the light to all the people you come in contact with, people who challenge you and are difficult, and those you love and care for. It is so abundant that you can now visualize it filling your neighborhood, your state, your country, all the countries and people of our world, and everything in it.

As you watch yourself and this pink light expanding ever outward, you may feel awe and amazement, knowing that this light began in you. As you continue expanding the pink light, it fills the universe as far as you can possibly imagine—every star, every planet, every atom, every molecule, and all the spaces in between. See the soft pink light bathing all things that ever were, that are, and that ever will be. See yourself as part of this great cosmos now glowing with pink light.

Stay in this experience as long as you wish to do so. Then slowly make your way back, still aware of what you have seen and felt, having touched the edge of this mystical level of consciousness. Know that you are part of the whole. The light that began in you is of the highest love. You are the vessel and a giver of this love. It is abundant, plentiful, limitless, and boundless. It is you, and it is yours. When you are ready, slowly come back to the room and open your eyes.

ENDNOTES

[1] J. E. Cirlot, *Dictionary of Symbols*, 2nd ed. (New York: Philosophical Library, Inc., 1983), 235.

This has been my favorite go-to book for symbols and metaphors. Each symbol has numerous explanations drawing on mythology or tradition from many different cultures. The way I use this book with patients is as follows: When a symbol arises, we look at all the entries for the symbol. Then I ask the patient to simply be aware of which ones resonate. In this way, we can most closely uncover what is meaningful to that person. I have used this book when synchronistic events occur—for instance, when an unusual animal shows up outside my office window or when we interpret dream imagery.

[2] Carl G. Jung, *Psychological Types*, trans. R. F. C. Hull, *The Collected Works of C.G. Jung* (Princeton: Princeton University Press, 1969), par. 757, 762.

[3] W. H. Murray, *The Scottish Himalaya Expedition* (London: J. M. Dent and Co., 1951).

[4] Carl G. Jung, *Synchronicity: An Acausal Connecting Principle* (Princeton, NJ: Princeton University Press, 1985) (Bollingen, Switzerland: Bollingen Foundation, 1993 [1952]).

[5] Lynea Weatherly, 1992.

I was first introduced to Lynea Weatherly in 1992 by a chiropractor who suggested I attend her workshop. She described herself as a psychic. Encounters with psychics were not new to me (in fact, I myself was once asked to be a "reader" by a metaphysical bookshop owner), but Lynea pushed my boundaries. In spite of the things that were a little "out there" even for me, I realized there was something of value in much of the content of her workshop. I have always appreciated her generosity in encouraging me and giving her blessings for letting me restructure and reword her Illume-a-Nation workshop so that I could teach it in the healthcare community. I called it Psy-Ki, short for psychological kinesiology.

[6] Hanna Pankowsky Davidson, *East of the Storm* (Lubbock: Texas Tech University Press, 2008).

My mother's autobiography documents her family's escape from Nazi-occupied Poland into Russia. We are very fortunate, perhaps because of my grandparents' intuition, that my grandfather, my grandmother, my uncle, and my mother were all spared the horror of being sent to a concentration camp and survived the war.

[7] "intuition," *New Oxford American Dictionary*, 2nd ed. Edited by Erin McKean (New York: Oxford University Press, 2005). Also available at http://www.oxfordamericandictionary.com/*Oxford English Dictionary*, Oxford University Press, 2014.

[8] I found a fascinating article on the internet entitled "Understanding Brainwaves" by Jeffery L. Fannin, PhD. It is a PDF white paper posted by Dr. Joe Dispenza. Although I could not find the date it was written or the other proper citation information, I refer you to it for a more in-depth exploration of brainwaves as discussed by a cutting edge neuroscientist.

[9] Mona Lisa Schulz, *Awakening Intuition* (New York: Three Rivers Press, 1998), 68–69.

I had the pleasure of meeting and attending a workshop with Mona Lisa Schulz in 1998. She is a brilliant and funny MD/PhD who became a wonderful role model by showing me how it is possible to be a doctor and an intuitive. This book has been my gold standard for describing and explaining some of the science behind intuition.

[10] Harry Wilmer, *Quest for Silence* (Einsiedeln, Switzerland: Daimon Verlag, 2000), 118–36; Harry Wilmer, unpublished material and in private conversation.

A man always ahead of his time, Dr. Wilmer was a prolific writer, publishing hundreds of papers and fifteen books. His books were unique in that he simplified complex ideas, often by the use of his original illustrations. Some of the titles he published are *Huber the Tuber* (written during a time when tuberculosis was rampant in order to help laypeople understand what it was), *Practical Jung: Nuts and Bolts of Jungian Psychology, Understanding Jung, How Dreams Help,* and *Quest for Silence.* While in the navy, he pioneered the treatment of war veterans with PTSD by using group therapy. His book about the work, *Social Psychiatry in Action,* became the subject of a 1961 docudrama called *People Need People,* starring Lee Marvin.

Dr. Wilmer was one of the first to recognize the drug problems that were arising in the sixties. He established the Youth Drug Ward, which served young hippies from the Haight-Ashbury district in San Francisco, people who had experienced adverse effects from drug use. The therapy included "creativity seminars," which featured such artists as Joan Baez and Rod Steiger. Also during the 1960s, Wilmer worked extensively with inmates from the San Quentin prison and their families. He continued his work with veterans while at the Audie Murphy VA Hospital in San Antonio.

When he retired from the University of Texas Health Science

Center at San Antonio in 1980, he established the Institute for the Humanities at Salado, where he hosted well-known people in the humanities, including artists, writers, scholars, scientists, and other speakers from every field to conduct workshops and give lectures. Recognizing the power and significance of these, I attended them from their inception, driving two hours twice a month during my medical school, internship, and residency. Often I was the youngest in the audience. Although I was shy at first, Dr. Wilmer encouraged an exchange and dialogue among all participants, so soon I was fully engaged and without hesitation. The opportunities to meet the extraordinary, creative, scholarly, and wise people in an intimate setting have been some of my most meaningful experiences. Many of the symposia arising from these extraordinary gatherings were also published as books, including *Mother Father*; *Vietnam in Remission*; *Facing Evil: Confronting the Dreadful Power of Genocide, Terrorism, and Cruelty*; and *Creativity, Paradoxes, and Reflections*.

Harry Wilmer was an insightful introvert and in his later years thought a great deal about silence. He was profoundly affected by a heart attack. He said that he realized the moment they stopped his heart during the procedure; it was the most complete experience of silence one could have, he reported. The result of his contemplations was *Quest for Silence*. On a lighter note, he also told me that he loved hearing aids because he could shut out noise any time he wanted by simply turning them off. He was a remarkable man, and I am grateful to have known him.

[11] Jimmy Durante (February 10, 1893–January 29, 1980).

It seemed odd that Jimmy Durante's nose showed up in this dream, especially since I was too young to have been a fan and had not seen much of his work. What strikes me is how the unconscious will nonetheless find such a perfect, clear image to create the pun and so get the message across.

[12] Thich Nah Hahn, *The Miracle of Mindfulness* (Boston, MA: Beacon Press Books, 1975).

This small book continues to be my favorite on mindfulness. Thich Nah Hahn is eloquent in the simplicity with which he writes. I especially like his comparison of the Western and the Eastern ways of eating a tangerine, found on page 5 of his book. The scenario he describes has remained vivid in my mind for years.

[13] Christine Page, MD. *Beyond the Obvious*, The C.W. Daniel Company Limited, 1998 and from personal interactions and workshops. Used with permission.

I first encountered Dr. Page at the 1998 NICABM and was so taken with the charming and insightful way she could talk and normalize the concepts and experience of intuition. Bringing in her European point of view, I could begin to understand how it would be possible to fully integrate all the alternative medicine methods with traditional ones. At the time these ideas were still relatively fringe so to hear how seamlessly they worked in England was a revelation. Later I attended her workshops where I continued to learn about intuition. She too became a role model and graciously permitted me to use some of her ideas here:

[14]©Helen Pankowsky MD, 2010. Inspired by Marianne Williamson.

[15] There are numerous books to learn about the chakras. Some of the ones I like are:

Rosalyn Bruyere, *Wheels of Light* (New York: Simon and Schuster, 1994).

Kalashatra Govinda, *Handbook of Chakra Healing* (Old Sayworth, CT: Konecky and Konecky, 2002).

Judith Anodea, *Wheels of Life* (St. Paul, MN: Llewellyn Publications, 1997).

Judith Anodea has also created an animated film that is quite beautiful. I use it in workshops for an effective visual, animated way of describing the chakras and the ascent of the kundalini energy.

For how chakras play a role in healing techniques, I refer you to:
Donna Eden, *Energy Medicine,* (New York: Jeremy P. Tarcher/Penguin, 1998, 2008).
Barbara Brennan, *Light Emerging,* (New York: Bantam Books, 1993).

[16] Claude Swanson, *Life Force, the Scientific Basis: Breakthrough Physics of Energy Medicine, Healing, Chi, and Quantum Consciousness* (Tucson, AZ: Poseidia Press, 2016); Claude Swanson, *The Synchronized Universe* (Tucson, AZ: Poseidia Press, 2003).

Dr. Swanson presented an eye-opening lecture at a Reiki training in Rochester, New York, in 2016, where he spoke on why and how healing energy works. His research and expertise go far beyond the information I learned from Dr. Hunt. I found his ideas exciting as quantum physics continues to illuminate more about the bioenergy field. He is a charming, unassuming person whom I teased about being a "rock star" to those of us who were his bioenergy groupies gathered at his lecture.

[17] Bruce Lipton, *The Biology of Belief* (New York: Hays House, 2005).

[18] Qian Quiroga, L. Reddy, G. Kreiman, C. Koch, and I. Fried. "Sounds of neurons firing," *Nature* no. 435 (2005): 1102–7.

Christof Koch, PhD, was kind and generous enough to send me the actual recordings of the neurons firing. It is astounding that we can hear this microcosmic event that is continuously occurring. I have used these recordings in my workshops.

[19] Valerie V. Hunt, *Music of Light* (Malibu: Malibu Publishing, 1993,

1998, and 1999); Valerie Hunt, private communications 1998–2013. The importance of the *Music of Light* was not the music but the recording of the sound of the aura/bioenergy field that is in the background. I once asked if she had just the raw recording without the music. She said she did but that she had no intention to ever release it, as it would be too powerful.

[20] Valerie V. Hunt, *Project Report: A Study of Structural Integration from neuromuscular, Energy Field, and Emotional Approaches.* Boulder, Colorado. Rolf Institute of Structural Integration (1977).

[21] Gaetan Chevalier, "The Biofield: What it is and why it is important to know about it" (ISSEEM Conference, Unity Village, MO, 2015), and in personal discussion.

As I was reeling from Valerie Hunt's death in 2014, Gaetan Chevalier was the first person I met who had known her and had actually worked on her instruments with her. I met him serendipitously (although there are no coincidences) in 2015 at the International Society for the Study of Subtle Energy and Energy Medicine (ISSEEEM) conference. It was heartening to know that through his research he was continuing to work on the creation of instruments that will measure the bioenergy-field emissions in the way that Dr. Hunt envisioned.

[22] Gerald Oster. "Auditory beats in the brain." *Scientific American* 229 no. 4 (1973): 94–102.

[23] I met Brian Dailey, MD and Sergey Sorin, MD when they conducted a workshop at the 2016 International Society for the Study of Subtle Energy and Energy Medicine (ISSSEEM) conference. This was my introduction to sound as medicine. I was impressed by the effects that this tool had. I experienced an acute clarity during guided meditations when combined with the auditory signals. I was also

impressed at the range of experiences that these two physicians, with robust emergency medicine practices, described in the use of this music/sound technology in the ERs.

[24] There is a rich library of research available on the topic of sound as treatment for medical conditions. For a very comprehensive list see The Monroe Institute web site. What follows are only a few references to get you started:

Brian Daily, Sergey Sorin, and Allyn Evans. "Sound medicine: Using state-of-the art technology to facilitate deep relaxation, sleep and pain management." *International Journal of Healing and Caring*, 2015.

Sergey Sorin and Brian Daily. "Sound Medicine: Western medicine meets complementary and alternative medicine to facilitate deep relaxation, sleep and pain management." *Journal of Comprehensive Integrative Medicine* 1 no. 2 (2016): 59–64.

Sergey Sorin. "Sound medicine facilitates deep relaxation, sleep and pain Management." *Journal of Green County Medical Society* 75 no. 8 (2016): 11, 13.

[25] Valerie Hunt, unpublished material.

One of the research projects that Dr. Hunt had enlisted me for was to study the correlation of bioenergy field, emotions, lifehoods, and cancer. Her hypothesis was based on the idea that people who tend to develop cancer have a biofield pattern of weakness in the lower frequency vibrations and hyperactivity in the high. This pattern reflects poor tissue health, fatigue, and tumor growth. The other variables she was exploring in this research were systemic oxygen deficiency and inflammation from hyperimmune activity. The assumption was that the biofield pattern reflected the blocked emotions related to survival. Her instruments would be the tangible measures of this biofield pattern. Although we had an oncologist, a staff, including a nutritionist, and myself as the psychiatrist, the research was never fully launched, since at the time we were poised to begin, Dr. Hunt became ill and subsequently passed away. She had not completed the instrument or developed the research that would allow us to carry on. Sadly, a few months later, our oncologist also passed away in a biking accident. It will be for someone else to carry on this type of research.

[26] Adapted from Valerie Hunt, *Mind Mastery Meditations* (Malibu, CA: Malibu Publishing, 1997), 52–55, and in conversation. Used with permission.

There is some controversy about the idea of the scalar wave, but Dr. Hunt was adamant in her belief that this was an effective method to store energy and use it for healing. Eventually it may prove to be the explanation for the storage of energy in the body that is used in martial arts.

[27] Valerie Hunt, personal communication, 2008–2014.

[28] ———. *Uncork Your Consciousness* (Malibu, CA: Malibu Publishing, 2008): 37.

[29] Roman Krznaric, "Roman Krznaric recommends the best books for the art of living." Interview. Audio blog post. *Five Books*, n.p. November 30, 2012. Retrieved from http://fivebooks.com/recommended/man's-search-meaning-by-viktor-e-frankl
——— . *How Should We Live? Great Ideas from the Past for Everyday Life* (Katonah: BlueBridge, 2013).

I first heard of this wise thinker while looking on the Internet, and I heard this podcast. Krznaric asked me to use the podcast as reference, but he has written these ideas in his books that I have also cited. He has written books and articles focusing on the important topic of compassion and empathy. If you want to see his cogent talk on empathy, I highly recommend *Outerspection*, an animated film on YouTube: https://www.youtube.com/watch?v=BG46IwVfSu8

[30] Sigmund Freud first described "repetition compulsion" in an article written in 1914, *"Erinnern, Wiederholen, und Durcharbeiten"* ("Remembering, Repeating, and Working Through") and later elaborated in "Beyond the Pleasure Principle," an essay written in 1920.

[31] Weixsue Su and his wife, Ming Xie, have been my tai chi teachers for more than a decade. Although remarkable as teachers, they have expressed humility about their skill levels, choosing to forgo the ranking system so common in the martial arts. Su will not allow himself to be referred to as a tai chi and qi gong master; rather he prefers the terms *teacher* or *scholar*. Over the years I have had numerous conversations with Su that have elucidated many of the philosophic principles of tai chi, qi gong, Taoism, and energy systems from the Eastern point of view. Our conversations about the *dantian* in particular helped me to formulate and see the correlations to the kundalini in the Hindu chakra system. He introduced me to the well-known diagram known as *nei jin tu* (internal meridian picture). The diagram is enlightening in that it depicts the chakras pictorially, by function. There are four connected yin-yangs and a farmer plowing the field with an ox representing the *dantian* and its function.

Tai chi has been very important to me for many years. I have learned to recognize and feel the energy flow in other people's bodies in healing, and I have learned to recognize and feel the energy flow in my own. Tai chi has also taught me how to intertwine the energy generated and flowing from my own body with all the energy that surrounds me outside of the body. The longer I practice, the more I come to understand how it is not only a physical or mental exercise, but a complete mind, body, spirit experience.

[32] Eknath Easwaran. *A Glossary of Sanskrit From the Spiritual Tradition of India*, Berkeley, Blue Mountain Center of Meditation, 1970, p.5.

[33] Paramahansa Yogananda. *Autobiography of a Yogi* (New York: The Philosophical Library, 1946).
Teri Degler (April 2012), "Hildegard of Bingen: A Yogini in Nun's Clothing," Institute for Consciousness Research.

[34] Joe Dispenza, *Becoming Supernatural* (New York: Hay House, 2017): 136.

[35] Jim B. Tucker (2000), "A scale to measure the strength of children's claims of previous lives: Methodology and initial findings," *Journal of Scientific Exploration* 14 (4): 571–81.

Dr. Tucker and his predecessor, Ian Stevens, MD, have conducted such excellent research that there is very little controversy around their work. I was thrilled to discover these two physicians and their work.

[36] Adapted from Valerie Hunt, *Uncork Your Consciousness* (Malibu, CA: Malibu Publishing, 2008).

[37] Adapted from Valerie Hunt, *Mind Mastery Meditations* (Malibu, CA: Malibu Publishing, 1997).

This book is Dr. Hunt's how-to manual with meditations to access the information in the mind-field. I have liberally borrowed from them with her permission. Although she felt these meditations were easy to do on one's own, I found that because we have so many blocks and resistances to making the mind information conscious, it is best to do these as guided imagery with someone else. I have often used these in my practice and workshops.

[38] Helen Pankowsky MD

I developed this exercise to use at the end of the classes and workshops I have taught. The pink color is a color symbolic of love. In some ways this exercise brings us back full circle to my introduction of this book. My intention is for you to have a similar experience as mine. An experience where, beginning with yourself, you can feel yourself expanding, reaching out, and touching the edge of the cosmos. In this way you may be able to realize that even you, as an individual, have power to affect the universe.

[39] ©Helen Pankowsky MD, 2010.

AUTHOR BIOGRAPHY

Helen Pankowsky, MD, considers herself a seeker, a healer, a teacher/student, first and secondly a doctor who specializes in psychiatry. With this in mind, she has devoted herself to integrating the best of traditional medicine with non-traditional modalities for optimal treatment of her patients and to teaching others how to maintain physical, emotional, and spiritual health.

Helen lives with her husband in San Antonio, Texas, where she works part time doing therapy and energy healing, teaches, reads, practices (plays) tai chi, writes poetry, and creates art. She continues to grow and explore the expanse of consciousness for herself while guiding patients, students, and anyone who desires to expand their awareness, helping them to embrace who they are and live their life to their highest potential.

Helen Pankowsky can be contacted at helen.inspiredlife@ gmail.com, www.helenpankowskymd.com, and her Facebook page, Inspired Life Psychiatry.

APPENDIX

Kinesiology, the Unconscious, and Limiting Decisions

For those who are interested, here is a brief description of the process that I called Psy-Ki.[39] Many details of this method have not been included as this is meant to be only a brief overview. (If you would like more information, please contact me at helen@ inspiredlifepsychiatry.com, www.helenpankowskymd.com, or Facebook.) In order for you to utilize this method, several assumptions have to be made, some involving a leap of faith:

1. We are energetic beings.

2. Just as some substances weaken the body, so too can thoughts and beliefs.

3. Substances, thoughts, and beliefs that are beneficial strengthen the body.

4. What is beneficial for the body/person elicits a yes answer; the muscle stays strong when resistance is applied to it. What weakens the body will elicit a no answer, and a muscle will yield with minimum pressure. You can test this right now. Stand up, close your eyes, ask your body to give you a yes, and just wait to see what your body does without any effort on your part. Chances are, you swayed forward (most people do, although a few might sway to one side or the other and some might even go backward). Now ask

for a no. Again, most people sway backward. It works the same if you ask someone to hold an arm up and to the side and then ask for a yes. Ask the person you are testing to resist your downward push, and try to press that person's arm down. The arm stays strong even with a fair amount of pressure. Now you ask for a no, again asking for the resistance from the other person. With minimal pressing on your part and even if the other tries very hard, the arm will easily go down. Any muscle group will work in the same way.

5. The body has seven strong energy centers traditionally called chakras. The first is the root, located between the legs. The second is at the pubis. The third is at the gut or the solar plexus. The fourth is the heart. The fifth is located at the throat. The sixth is the space between the eyebrows or the third eye, and the seventh is the crown or on top of the head.

6. In this system the centers represent aspects of our human-ness, from the most physical to the most spiritual. The first center represents the body and our physical existence; the second, our cultural identity; the third, our self-esteem; the fourth, our capacity to love; the fifth our ability to express knowledge and creativity or the authentic voice; the sixth, our intuition; and the seventh, our spiritual connectedness to the divine.

7. Each center is defined by specific words corresponding to its representation, giving each center a series of words that can then be muscle tested one at a time in the form of a question. The testing must be done through questions only, as the inherent limitation is that of yes/no answers. The words that test strong are then grouped to form a question.

For example, let's say that the word "woman" in the second center and the phrase "speak your truth" in the fifth center tested strong, while all the other words tested weak. If so, the question would be this: "As a woman, can you speak your truth?" This would be tested and, if it is a limiting decision or part of the programming/beliefs that weaken, it will test weak.

8. After determining through questioning that the person has a willingness to change, then the "Meditation for Transformation" is done—a reprogramming of sorts. The meditation consists of seven components that are visualizations. The visualization aligns what I referred to at the time as the physical energy field, the emotional energy field, and the spiritual energy field. I now refer to this as the bioenergy field/mind-field. We are electromagnetic beings and are surrounded by these fields. I concede that how this alignment occurs requires the biggest "leap of faith." I tried to find explanations for each step in the Meditation for Transformation. I could not find any good way to explain the alignment. Keep in mind that this was before I knew much about the bioenergy field and mind-field, so I had no model to follow at the time. Even though now I can explain how the energy field may be aligned when it is flowing coherently, there is still a factor that I call the "mystery," which simply must be taken into account.

And here is where the "magic" happens. After doing this meditation/visualization, the same question is again tested, and it tests strong. Every time that same question is tested, it will continue to stay strong.

Ways of Muscle Testing Using Kinesiology

Testing with a pendulum:

"Yes" turns clockwise   "No" turns counterclockwise

Self-testing by holding hand with fingers outstretched, press in at pinkie and forefinger. "Yes" stays strong. "No" is weak and will fold in.

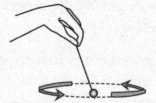

Self-testing by interlocking the thumb and forefinger of both hands and then pulling in opposite directions. "Yes" stays strong. "No" will be weak and easily pull away.

Self-testing using "the sway": "Yes" is usually a frontward sway. "No" is usually a backward sway.

Testing others: Tester pushes down on arm. "Yes" stays strong and doesn't move. "No" is weak and easily gives.

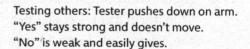

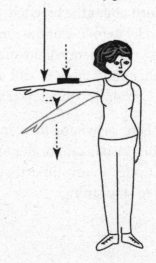

Kinesiology is a useful tool for getting yes/no answers from the unconscious via the body, but it is a very limited information-obtaining technique. Using the pendulum, the yes/no is determined by whether the pendulum moves in a clockwise or counterclockwise direction. Do not confuse the direction of the spin with coherency and anticoherency. Usually yes is clockwise while no is counterclockwise. There are many ways to do kinesiology. What follows are some examples:

1. *Hand Self-Testing.* In the first way, one hand is held stretched out (the hand being used for testing) while the other pushes against the forefinger and pinky of the tested hand. A yes will meet strong resistance, while a no will be weak, and the fingers of the tested hand will come together. In the second, the two hands are held with the forefingers and thumbs closed but in an interlocking position, as though making a link. When there is an attempt to pull them apart, the yes will stay strong while the no will easily be pulled apart.

2. *The Sway.* This is the easiest and least strenuous way of self-testing. You simply stand still, relax, close your eyes (if you wish to do so), and ask for a yes. Allow your body to move on its own. Most often you will sway forward without thinking of it. With a no, most people sway backward.

3. *Testing Others.* There are many ways to test others. I am including only one, but any opposing muscle movement will work the same. In this technique, the person being tested stands with his or her arm outstretched. The person testing applies pressure downward on that arm, while the person being tested resists that pressure (pushing against the tester). A yes will stay strong, while a no will not be able to resist, and the arm will easily come down.

Kinesiology can be used in many ways. Essentially it is a simplistic way of getting information from the unconscious, the mind-field, or other energy systems. It can be used in the way it was originally intended, which is to get information from the body, such as which vitamin of all the ones on the shelf might be best for you. However, it should never be used to make medical diagnoses or judgments about the body or illness. Nor should it be used instead of medical opinion on treatments.

Kinesiology can be used for the following:

- Obtaining information that the body knows

- Obtaining information from any energy system

- Communicating with the unconscious mind

Kinesiology cannot be used for the following:

- Making judgments or important decisions

- Predicting the future

- As a sole diagnostic tool (I don't recommend using it in Las Vegas either!)

References

Alexander, Eben. *Proof of Heaven*. New York: Simon and Schuster, 2012.

Anodea, Judith. *Wheels of Life*. St. Paul, MN: Llewellyn Publications, 1987.

Bolen, Jean Shinoda. *The Tao of Psychology*, New York: Harper Collins, 1979.

Brennan, Barbara Ann. *Hands of Light*. New York: Bantam Books, 1988.

Brennan, Barbara Ann. *Light Emerging*. New York: Bantam Books, 1993.

Bruyere, Rosalyn. *Wheels of Light*. New York: Simon and Schuster, 1994.

Cameron, Julia. *The Artist's Way*. New York: Jeremy P. Tracher/Putnam, 1992.

Chalmers, David. *The Conscious Mind: In Search of a Fundamental Theory*. New York: Oxford University Press, 1997.

Chen, Zhenglei. *Chen's Tai Chi for Health and Wellness*. Ontario, Canada: White Bench Publications, 2010.

Chevalier, Gaetan. *The Biofield: What It Is and Why It Is Important to Know about It*. Unity Village, MO: ISSEEM Conference, 2015.

Chevalier, Gaetan. Private communication at the International Society for the Study of Subtle Energy and Energy Medicine conference and email, 2015.

Cirlot, J. E. *Dictionary of Symbols*. 2nd ed. New York: Philosophical Library, 1983, 235.

Conrad, Emilie. *Life on Land*. Berkeley, CA: North Atlantic Books, 2007.

Daily, Brian MD FACEP, FACFE, Sergey Sorin MD, DABFM and Allyn Evans, MBA. "Sound Medicine: Using State-Of-The Art technology to facilitate deep relaxation, sleep and pain management." *International Journal of Healing and Caring*, September 1, 2015.

Day, Laura. *Practical Intuition*. Toronto/New York: Random House/Villard Books, 1996.

Degler, Teri. "Hildegard of Bingen: A Yogini in Nun's Clothing." Institute for Consciousness Research, April, 2012.

Dispenza, Joe. *Becoming Supernatural*, New York: Hay House, 2017.

Easwaran, Eknath. *A Glossary of Sanskrit from the Spiritual Tradition of India*. Berkeley, CA: Blue Mountain Center of Meditation, 1970.

Eden, Donna. *Energy Medicine*. London: Penguin Putnam, 1998.

Emery, Marcia. *Intuitive Healer*. Upper Saddle River, NJ: Prentice-Hall, 1994.

Emery, Marcia. *Intuition Workbook*. Upper Saddle River, NJ: Prentice-Hall, 1994.

Frankl, Viktor. *Man's Search for Meaning*. Boston, MA: Beacon Press, 1959.

Gladwell, Malcolm. *Blink*. New York: Little, Brown and Company, 2005.

Govinda, Kalashatra. *Handbook of Chakra Healing*. Old Sayworth, CT: Konecky and Konecky, 2004.

Gopi Krishna. *The Awakening of the Kundalini*. Markdale, ON: The Institute for Consciousness Research and The Kundalini Research Foundation, Ltd. 2014.

Hanh, Thich Nhat. *The Miracle of Mindfulness*. Boston, MA: Beacon Press Books, 1975.

Horgan, John. *Rational Mysticism*. Boston, MA: Houghton Mifflin, 2003.

Hunt, Valerie. *Bioscalar: The Primary Healing Energy*. CD. Malibu, CA: Malibu Publishing, 2008.

Hunt, Valerie. *Infinite Mind*. Malibu, CA: Malibu Publishing, 1996.

Hunt, Valerie. *Mind Mastery Meditations*. Malibu, CA: Malibu Publishing, 1997.

Hunt, Valerie. Music *of Light*. CD. Malibu, CA: Malibu Publishing, 1993, 1998, 1999.

Hunt, Valerie. *New Annotated Glossary*. Malibu, CA: Malibu Publishing, 2011.

Hunt, Valerie. *Scientist to Mystic: Journey of a Soul*. Malibu, CA: Malibu Publishing, 2008.

Hunt, Valerie. *Splendifferent*. Malibu, CA: Malibu Publishing, 2011.

Hunt, Valerie. *Uncork Your Consciousness*. Malibu, CA: Malibu Publishing, 2008.

Hunt, Valerie. *Project Report: A Study of Structural Integration from neuromuscular, Energy Field, and Emotional Approaches.* Boulder, CO: Rolf Institute of Structural Integration, 1977.

Hunt, Valerie. Workshops, unpublished material, and private communications, 1998–2013. All used by permission.

Jou, Tsung Hwa. *The Tao of Tai-Chi Chuan: Way to Rejuvenation.* New York: Tai Chi Foundation, 1991.

Jung, Carl G. "Forerunners of the Idea of Synchronicity." *The Collected Works of C.G. Jung.* Vol. 8. Translated by R.F.C. Hull, 485–531. Princeton, NJ: Princeton University Press, 1969.

Jung, Carl G. *Synchronicity: An Acausal Connecting Principle.* Princeton, NJ: Princeton University Press, 1985.

Jung, Carl G. "Tavistock Lectures-Lecture 1." *The Collected Works of C.G.Jung.* Vol. 18. Translated by R. F. C. Hull, 34. Princeton, NJ: Princeton University Press.

Koch, Christof, KLAB, Cal Tech. Private communications about sound of neurons firing, 2008–2009.

Krznaric, Roman. "Have You Tried the Six Varieties of Love?" *Sojourners Magazine,* Web edition Dec. 5, 2013. https://sojo.net/articles/have-you-tried-six-varieties-love

Krznaric, Roman. *How Should We Live? Great Ideas from the Past for Everyday Life.* Katonah, NY: BlueBridge, 2013.

Krznaric, Roman. "Roman Krznaric Recommends the Best Books for the Art of Living." Interview. Audio blog post. *Five Books.* N.p. November 30, 2012. Accessed September 16, 2014. http://fivebooks.com/recommended/man's-search-meaning-by-viktor-e-frankl. Interview.

Lahl, Suzanne. Workshops and consultations in Denver, 2003; Hawaii, 2005; Orange County, 2006. Used by permission.

Lahl, Suzanne. Unpublished materials and private communications, 1998 to present. Used by permission.

Liebman, Joshua Loth. *Peace of Mind*. New York: Simon and Schuster, 1946.

Lipton, Bruce. *The Biology of Belief 10th Anniversary Edition*. New York: Hays House, 2015.

Monroe, Robert. *Journeys Out of the Body (1st ed.)*. Garden City, NY: Doubleday, 1971.

Monroe, Robert. *Far Journeys* (1st ed.). Garden City, NY: Doubleday, 1985.

Monroe, Robert. *Ultimate Journey* (1st ed.). Garden City, NY: Doubleday, 1994.

Murray, W. H. *The Scottish Himalaya Expedition*. London: J. M. Dent NS Co., 1951.

Myss, Caroline. *Anatomy of the Spirit*. New York: Harmony Books, 1996, and in classes.

Nadel, Laurie. *Dr. Laurie Nadel's Sixth Sense*. Lincoln, NE: ASJA Press, 2006.

Naparesteck, Belleruth. *Your Sixth Sense: Unlocking the Power of Intuition*. New York: HarperCollins, 1997.

Narrin, Janeanne. *One Degree Beyond: A Reiki Journey into Energy Medicine*. Seattle, WA: Little White Buffalo Publishing Cottage, 1998.

Ober, Clinton, Stephen T. Sinatra, and Martin Zucker. *Earthing*.

Laguna Beach, CA: Basic Health Publications, 2010.

Orloff, Judith. *Second Sight*. New York: Warner Books, 1997.

Oster, Gerald (October 1973). "Auditory beats in the brain." *Scientific American*, 229 (4): 94–102.

Page, Christine. *Beyond the Obvious*. Ashingdon, Essex, England: C. W. Daniel Co., Ltd., 1998.

Page, Christine. *Mirror of Existence*. Ashingdon, Essex, England: C. W. Daniel Co. Ltd., 1995.

Page, Christine. Workshops, classes, and private communications, 1997–2012. Used by permission.

Pankowsky Davidson, Hanna. *East of the Storm*. Lubbock, TX: Texas Tech University Press, 2008.

Yogananda, Paramahansa. *Autobiography of a Yogi*. New York: The Philosophical Library, 1946.

Yogananda, Paramahansa. *The Second Coming of Christ: The Resurrection of the Christ Within You*. Los Angeles: Self-Realization Fellowship Publishers, 1980.

Parnia, Sam. *Erasing Death*. New York: HarperCollins, 2013.

Quiroga, Rodrigo Quian, Leila Reddy, Gabriel Kreiman, Christof Koch, and Itszhak Fried. "Sounds of Neurons Firing." *Nature* 435 (2005): 1102–1107.

Remen, Rachel Naomi. *Kitchen Table Wisdom*. New York: Riverhead Trade, 1996.

Remen, Rachel Naomi. *My Grandfather's Blessing*. New York: Riverhead Trade, 2001.

Remen, Rachel Naomi. Interview on "Speaking of Faith with Krista Tippett." American Public Media, 2007.

Rosenoff, Nancy. *Intuition Workout*. Fairfield, CT: Aslan Publishers, 1991.

Schulz, Mona Lisa. *Awakening Intuition*. New York: Three Rivers Press, 1998.

Schulz, Mona Lisa. *The New Feminine Brain*. New York: Free Press, 2005.

Schwartz, Jeffrey M. *The Mind and the Brain: Neuroplasticity and the Power of Mental Force*. New York: Regan Books, HarperCollins, 2002.

Segaller, Steven and Berger, Merrill. *The Wisdom of the Dream*. Boston, MA: Shambhala, 1989.

Shealy, C. Norman. *Medical Intuition*. Virginia Beach, VA: A.R.E. Press, 2010.

Shroder, Tom. *Old Souls*. New York: Simon and Schuster Paperbacks, 1999.

Siegel, Daniel J. *The Mindful Brain: Reflection and Attunement in the Cultivation of Well-being*. New York: WW Norton and Company, 2007.

Sorin, Sergey and Brian Daily. "Sound Medicine: Western medicine meets complementary and alternative medicine to facilitate deep relaxation, sleep and pain management." *Journal of Comprehensive Integrative Medicine*, 1 (2): 59– 64, 2016.

Sorin, Sergey and Brian Daily. "Sound Medicine Facilitates Deep Relaxation, Sleep and Pain Management." *Journal of Green County Medical Society*, 75 (8): 11, 13, 2016.

Stein, Diane. *The Essential Reiki*. Berkeley, CA: The Crossing Press, Inc., 1997.

Swanson, Claude. *Life Force, the Scientific Basis: Breakthrough Physics of Energy Medicine, Healing, Chi, and Quantum Consciousness*. Tucson, AZ: Poseidia Press, 2009.

Swanson, Claude. *The Synchronized Universe*. Tucson, AZ: Poseidia Press, 2016.

Tucker, James. *Life before Life*. New York: St. Martin's Press, 2005.

Tucker, James. "A Scale to Measure the Strength of Children's Claims of Previous Lives: Methodology and Initial Finding." *Journal of Scientific Exploration* 14 (4): 571–81, 2000.

Vaughan, Frances. *Awakening Intuition*. New York: Anchor Books, 1979.

Weatherly, Lynea. *"Illume-a-Nation."* Workshop, San Antonio, Texas, 1993.

Wilmer, Harry. Lectures. Unpublished material and private communications, 1981–2004.

Wilmer, Harry. *Quest for Silence*. Switzerland: Daimon Verlag, 2000.

Zdenek, Marilee. *The Right Brain Experience*. New York: McGraw-Hill Book Company, 1986.

Zdenek, Marilee. Unpublished material, 1985.

Zion, Tina. *Become A Medical Intuitive*. WriteLife Publishing, 2012.

Zion, Tina. *Advanced Medical Intuition*. WriteLife Publishing, 2018.